THE

OHIO RAILROAD GUIDE:

ILLUSTRATED AND DESCRIPTIVE,

CONTAINING

TOPOGRAPHICAL, BIOGRAPHICAL, AND STATISTICAL NOTICES OF THE COUNTIES, TOWNS, AND SCENERY,--WITH BRIEF SKETCHES OF PUBLIC MEN:

BEING A

TRAVELLING COMPANION THROUGH OHIO.

CINCINNATI:
CINCINNATI GAZETTE COMPANY PRINT.
1852.

THE

OHIO RAILROAD GUIDE:

ILLUSTRATED AND DESCRIPTIVE.

PART I.

Cincinnati, Hamilton & Dayton Railway,

AND

MAD RIVER AND LAKE ERIE RAILWAY

FROM DAYTON TO SPRINGFIELD.

CINCINNATI:
CINCINNATI GAZETTE COMPANY PRINT.
1852.

GUIDE BOOK.

CINCINNATI, HAMILTON, AND DAYTON RAILROAD.

	Distance from Cincinnati.	Intermediate Distance.	Distance from Dayton.
Cincinnati			60
Cumminsville	5	5	55
Spring Grove	7	2	53
Ludlow	8	1	52
Carthage	10	2	50
Lockland	12	2	48
Glendale	15	3	45
Jones'	19	4	41
Hamilton	25	6	35
Busenback's	30	5	30
Trenton	33	3	27
Middletown.	37	4	23
Post Town	40	3	20
Carlisle	44	4	16
Miamisburgh	49	5	11
Carrolton	52	3	8
Dayton	60	8	

DISTANCES FROM DAYTON TO SPRINGFIELD.

To Enon . . . . 17 miles.
" Hotskin's Mills . . . . 19 "
" Water Station . . . . 20½ "
" Deep Cut . . . . 21½ "
" Crossing of National Road . . . . 23 "
" Springfield . . . . 24 "

FROM SPRINGFIELD TO SANDUSKY . . . . 134 "

DAYTON AND GREENVILLE RAILROAD.

	Distance. from Dayton.	Intermediate Distance.	Distance from Greenville.
Dayton			35
Higgins	6	6	29
Brookville	12	6	23
Junction.	15	3	20
Baltimore.	18	3	17
Gordon	21	3	14
Arcanum	26	5	9
Jay	30	4	5
Greenville	35	5	

HAMILTON AND EATON RAILROAD.

	Distance from Hamilton.	Intermediate Distance.	Distance from Eaton.
Hamilton			27
Seven Mile	7	7	20
Collinsville	11	4	16
Summerville	14	3	13
Camden	19	5	8
Eaton	27	8	

GUIDE BOOK

OF

THE OHIO RAILWAYS.

CINCINNATI.

CINCINNATI is one of the Wonders of the West. Seventy years ago, on the site where now is the fifth city of the United States, exhibiting all the evidence of high civilization,—there was a lonely forest, in the midst of which appeared a few solitary mounds,—remains of an unknown people. Such a contrast is nowhere to be found; those cities of our country which are larger in size, or equally rapid in growth, are all of older date. None of so recent origin have such strength and magnitude. It is here, then, that we find one of the most striking examples of rapid development, from the Savage to the Civilized state. The natural scenery around,—hills, river and plain, are all associated, even in the memory of a single life, with the extremes of the wild forest, in the Past, and the thick populated city of the Present.

At the close of the Revolution, the site of Cincinnati was on the war path of the Shawnees, and other Indian tribes, as they passed from their settlements on the Scioto and Miamis to the interior of Kentucky. The mouth of the Licking, opposite Cincinnati, was a land mark on their route. There, also assembled, in 1780, the army of General CLARKE, in the first successful expedition against the Indians of the Scioto, at Chil-li-co-the, and Pickaway. It was from a volunteer in that army,—a celebrated pioneer,—SIMON KENTON,—that the county which contains the city of Covington, was recently named. Where Cincinnati is, there was not then even an Indian village. The only works of man seen amidst the solitary forests, were those mysterious mounds and solitary ramparts, which indicated a once populous country, but of whose people and character,—not a remnant, nor a tradition remains. Lofty trees had grown and fallen upon them, when the Shawnee pursued his enemies on the war path of the Licking; but no voice from those ancient tombs told by whom, or for what they were raised! The shadows of Time flitted over them, and Mystery returned no answer to the questions of Curiosity; the Indians seem to have simply regarded them as monuments, and beyond that, to have had little interest in them.

After the settlement of Cincinnati, some curious young men opened one of the mounds, but found little, except human bones, some pieces of copper, lead, and coal, and some very rude sculpture.* These monuments and works were situated in the very heart of the present city. One mound stood at the corner of Main and Third streets,—the most valuable lot in the town; another was on Fifth street, below Western Row. Between Walnut and Race, Third and Fifth streets, was one of those circular ramparts, or fortifications, as they are usually called,—so frequently found among the ancient remains of the West; another was between Broadway and Sycamore, near Fourth. These works seem to prove that Cincinnati was, in days beyond memory, what it now is: the populous residence of the then occupants of Ohio. But between that period, and that of the white settlers, darkness rests upon all surrounding objects. We know that the forest has grown up on these works of an ancient people; and that the city has again replaced the forest, and on the ruins of the monuments, built the marts of commerce, and the abodes of civilization; but of the shadowy space between, we have neither history, tradition, nor memory.

It was nearly ten years after George Rogers Clarke and Simon Kenton had crossed the mouth of the Licking on their victorious march to the Shawnese towns of the Scioto, that a small band of sixteen persons left Maysville, (then called Limestone,) for the present Cincinnati. It was in the cold month of December, 1788. The sky was dark, the river was filled with running ice, and the shores lowered with inhospitable savages. Such scenes, and dangers, however, were familiar to the bold pioneers, and after two or three days struggling in the ice, Ludlow and his companions landed safely opposite the Licking. The spot, now Cincinnati, was within the patent of John

* Drake's "Picture of Cincinnati," 1815.

CLEVES SYMMES, who, in the year previous, had issued a pamphlet, proclaiming the future settlement of this country, and that such was the amazing fertility of the land, he actually believed, it was worth a silver dollar per acre! Attracted by such representations, MATTHIAS DENMAN, of New Jersey, purchased an interest in "Symmes' Grant," and "located" the section and fractional section, (about eight hundred acres,) on which Cincinnati is now built. He then sold them to PATTERSON and FILSON, and in August, 1788, they agreed to lay out a town. Soon after this, however, FILSON, who had come out to Kentucky, was killed by the Indians, and his share transferred to ISRAEL LUDLOW, who thus became the first leader, and pioneer, among the settlers of Cincinnati.

It was a cold season, and Nature was clad in her wildest array, when his little band landed amidst forest trees, under the shadow of those olden mounds. But there was no shadow on their mind. They dreamed of a beautiful future; a town to be built on lands that were positively worth a silver dollar per acre, * must certainly make the fortunes of all who first adventured within its golden precincts. In their dreams there was something of the ludicrous, as well as the sublime. Before they set out from the sands of New Jersey, the town of their imagination must have a *name*! FILSON, one of the original three in the project, was a schoolmaster, and his genius was appealed to for the much wanted name. The appeal was not in vain; he gave a name in August, 1788,—before the settlers had left their homes,—which was at once unique and *original*. He called the embryo town LOSANTIVILLE! This name, on being analyzed, is supposed to be made up of four different languages, namely: "L," (Licking,) English,—*os*, Greek,—*anti*, Latin,—and *ville*, French! It signifies "The town opposite the mouth of the Licking," and by this name is spoken of by Judge SYMMES. It seems, however, never to have been given to the real town, for when LUDLOW came to survey and record the village, it was called CINCINNATI.† It commenced with half a dozen log cabins, and in 1796,—seven years after,—was still composed of log cabins, and perhaps a dozen rough frame houses, with stone chimneys. Not a brick had been seen in the place.

---

* BURNET'S Letters.

† Ibid.

In June, 1789, Major DOUGHTY of the United States Army, arrived at Cincinnati, and commenced the erection of a block house, called "FORT WASHINGTON," which gave the first impulse to the settlement, and was the rendezvous of the army and the United States officers during the next ten or fifteen years. The early settlers naturally collected around it for safety and society, during the war of the North West. The times were wild and dangerous, but in the "Fort," as in the old Feudal Castle, the brave and adventurous spirits dispelled all thoughts of gloom, in the bowl, the song, or the dance. Many a gallant soldier and courteous gentleman, many a refined and elegant lady, gave as much of charm and zest to this camp in the wilderness, as if it had been a court in Europe. Here the high-minded ST. CLAIR, the heroic WAYNE, the young and impulsive HARRISON, and the fascinating WILKINSON, and others since conspicuous in history,—formed a delightful circle, enjoying the pleasures of intellectual and cheerful converse. Much of the history and spirit of that time may be found in the "Letters" of Judge BURNET,—who, having mingled in those scenes and events, yet survives to see the Metropolis of the West sprung up, dream-like, where the mound, the forest, and the Fort once stood!

FORT WASHINGTON.

"FORT WASHINGTON" was on the brow of the slight hill, separating the upper from the lower plain of the town, and where Third street now runs from Broadway to Ludlow street. The front parapet was a little south of the south line of Third, and the flag-staff was placed at just about the intersection of Third and Ludlow. From 1790 to the Greenville treaty, 1795, the settlers were obliged to keep close within, or near the defences of the fort; for the whole neighborhood was scoured with hostile Indians. They watched from the tops of the surrounding hills. Mount Adams, where the Observatory now is,—just to the north-east of the site of Fort Washington,—was then an Observatory for the Indians, as it now is to the Astronomers. On its top was a large and magnificent oak; in that tree,—WHITE EYES, an Indian chief, subsequently told a lady in the fort,—he had often watched, concealed by its foliage, the operations of the Garrison. He could see every motion, and knew everything that was going on. Men were cut down in the very precincts of the garrison, and the woods resounded with the war whoop of the savage, and the wails of the dying. These dangers, however, did not last long. The treaty of Greenville, following the victory of WAYNE, terminated the conflict. Peace restored the hopes, and commenced the prosperity of Cincinnati. In 1805, an emigration from Baltimore gave a new impulse to the town, and in 1807, the Surveyor General of the United States surveyed into lots the sixteen acres which had been reserved by the Government around Fort Washington, and they were sold to individuals, at public auction. Strangers who walk up the well built and spacious "Broadway,"—a noble street,—perceive that at Fourth street it is narrowed down to the common width, and frequently ask "why was this; why not continue this broad avenue through the town?" The truth is, it is only due to the government that there was any street of such breadth. The Fort Washington Reservation extended from the river, east of the public quay, to Fourth street, and its western boundary was Broadway,—which the Surveyor General voluntarily made one hundred feet broad.

The sale of Fort Washington and its lands, in lots, may be said to terminate the primitive or pioneer period of Cincinnati. Time enough has passed since, (brief as it is in comparison with that of older cities,) to make the reminiscences of that period interesting, and cause its memorials to be gathered up and looked upon as antiquities! The races of the Mounds and Forts were ancient and extinct hundreds of years ago. The race of Red Men, old long since,—are gone,—scarcely remembered and almost unknown to the present inhabitants. And now the Pioneers of yesterday are ancient; their grave-yards are removed, their dwellings have disappeared, their traditions are sought out, and the stately mansions of ease and elegance rise where the log cabin and the rough frame once were:

"Time rolls his ceaseless course. The race of yore,
Who danced our infancy upon their knee,
And told our marvelling boyhood legend's store
Of their strange ventures, happed by land or sea,
How are they blotted from the things that be!"

Of the Pioneer period of Cincinnati, enough has been preserved in various accounts, to give a very vivid and distinct picture of its appearance, manners, and growth. As we walk round the city, the natural turn of the grounds, the curved hills, the flowing river, and even the present streets, are all so associated with what was the Cincinnati of 1790-1800, and what it now is, that the story can be read as we go. It is true that the ancient mounds are obliterated; of Fort Washington there is no trace; that the alder swamps on the hill are forgotten, the shades of Deer Creek faded like fairy dreams, and the graves of Pioneers surmounted with the spires of lofty churches, and the splendid marts of merchandize. But yet the ground and the original plat of the town remain, and we can retrace the faded picture with the colors of memory.

Deer Creek, of which we spoke, is on the east side of the town, and winds round the base of Mount Adams, from whose summit the Observatory is visible from every quarter. The traveller who arrives by the Little Miami Railroad, seeks out the creek, and sees the outlet of the State's Miami Canal having its other extreme at Toledo, on Lake Erie, but looks in vain for the creek. The creek is carried through an arched culvert, the earth is filled up over, and dwellings and work shops surmount. He crosses the mouth on a stone bridge, and usually hastens by an omnibus, along Second street, (Columbia,) to one of the principal hotels. In doing this, he crosses what is called the "Third Ward," included between Third street and the river, on the lower plain. Nearly every foot of this space is now actively employed in business, but the stranger will be surprised to learn, it was originally, for the most part, a pond. The pond was frozen in winter, and on its ice, the few boys of the town found sport in skating, while in the spring, the wild duck floated on its bosom! Above, (on Third street,) was Fort Washington, while the pond stretched from Broadway to Deer Creek, below, and the principal part of the town was between Broadway and Main street. Deer Creek, a small rivulet, along whose banks the Miami Canal may now be seen, was enveloped, on the surrounding slopes, with a dense forest. In the Spring floods, the boys would go up the little stream in canoes, and gather flowers, or throw clubs at the turtles sunning themselves on logs. Near Pike street, where are now the fine mansion and beautiful gardens of NICHOLAS LONGWORTH, Esq. "on the very spot where the people now go to watch the unfolding of the night blooming cereus,—grew the red bud, crab apple, and gigantic tulip tree, or yellow poplar, with wild birds above, and native flowers below."* Proceeding, on the lower plain of the city, by Second, or Front streets, we arrive in succession, at Broadway, Sycamore, and Main streets, in front of what is now the Public Landing. The landing, which is now so finely paved, and gently graded, and which is crowded with the materials of commerce, had then no existence. The *common* stretched out to the natural bank of the river, which was high, steep, and crumbling. Under it were moored the flat-boats, or "arks" of the river traders, who came from Fort Pitt, Wheeling, and other towns, to dispose of their apples, flour, or whisky, below. On Front street, near the corner of Sycamore, was the "Tavern" of GRIFFIN YEATMAN, Esq., the first hotel keeper of Cincinnati! This worthy man lived to within two or three years since,—was long Recorder of the county, and died respected,—having nearly spanned, in his single life, the whole existence of Cincinnati!

This hotel often received distinguished guests, whose business or curiosity led them through the wilds of the West. In 1796, Judge BURNET relates,† he met there the celebrated writer and traveller, VOLNEY, who had traversed Kentucky on foot, and carried his wardrobe in an oil cloth! He afterwards published

*DRAKE'S Discourse.
† BURNET'S Letters.

his observations, accompanied by philosophical reflections on the region of the Ohio.

Opposite the mouth of Sycamore street, near YEATMAN's hotel, "There was a small wooden market house, built over a cove, into which pirogues and other craft, when the river was high, were poled, or paddled, to be tied to the rude columns."* In Main street, below the hill, were a few shops; and it was not uncommon to see the wolf or panther brought in by the hunters; or, occasionally, as wild men of the woods, looking with curiosity on the habitations and movements of the new invaders of their land.

If the stranger now takes his course from the bottom to the upper plain, by way of Broadway, he will see that the city now covers nearly all the upper plain, and the houses begin to ascend the sides, and crown the tops of the hills. But in the days of which we speak, there was scarcely a house in all that region. Alone, and surrounded by a garden and open fields, was the house of WINTHROP SARGENT, Esq., Secretary of the North West Territory, standing on, or near, what is now Macalister street. On the other side of Broadway, between Third and Fourth, where are now the elegant mansions of Messrs. SHOENBERGER, LAWLER, and others, was a corn field, surrounded by a corn-field fence. Pursuing our way down Fourth street, where now the traveller sees the tallest spire in the United States, and asks "What church is that?" was the first graveyard,—where

> "Each in his narrow cell forever laid,
> The rude forefathers of the hamlet slept."

Not *sleep* as the poet has it, for in less than a generation since the first rude church was there erected, the bones of its founders have either been removed by their surviving relatives, or scattered to the winds by thoughtless strangers! It is but a few years since, when the workmen were digging the cellars of the houses at the North East corner of Fourth and Walnut streets, large quantities of human bones were disinterred,—no friend near to recognize them, and neither stone or history to tell who they were!

The square between Main and Walnut, Fourth and Fifth streets, was originally dedicated as a Public Square. Within

* BURNET's Letters.

FIRST CHURCH BUILT IN CINCINNATI.

the angle of Main and Fourth, where the First Presbyterian Church now stands, was erected the first, and at the time we refer to, the only church of the village of Cincinnati. It was a small frame house, and in rear of it, near Walnut street, stood, some years after, a frame school house. In process of time, as this was a "public square," the County Commissioners took possession of the north half, on Fifth street, and there erected a Court House and Jail,—both, we believe, made of logs. As time advanced, the school was erected into a college, and finally, the large stone building fronting Walnut street, and occupied by the Mercantile Library Association, and Merchants' Exchange, was built on the school lot. The Public Square thus come into the possession of three corporations,—the First Presbyterian Society, the College, and the County Commissioners. The *citizens*, to whom the square properly belonged, lost their rights by non-usance. The County Commissioners removed the Court House, and *leased the lots;* the Church did the same on the Main and Fourth street sides,—reserving its own premises on the interior ground; the College built the Walnut street front, and thus, what was intended for a fresh green, pleasant to the tired citizen, has been covered with stores and shops. This *possession* was gradually acquired, so that when the citizens began to wake from their slumber, it was too late to regain their right. A long controversy ensued, which was decided against the city, by lapse of time. In the proceedings, depositions of old settlers were taken, which embody and make permanent, the early history of the town.

In the midst of this square, where the old church stood, rises the lofty spire of the new church, stretching 280 feet into the sky, and offering to such as are able to attain its upper part, a most picturesque and splendid view of the surrounding city.

But we must return to our walk within the ancient village of 1800, which, in the darkness of that profound antiquity, (!) seems to us something like Nineveh, as we endeavor to disinter the mounds, forts, and ancient temples!

As the stranger walks two or three squares further, he will see the slender towers,—imitations of the minarets, or some strange architecture,—which belong to the Mechanics' Institute, on the corner of Sixth and Vine streets. This building is on the highest lot of the city, and from the hills seems to stand out in bold relief. "There," says Dr. DRAKE, "was part of a wheat field of sixteen acres, owned by Mr. JAMES FERGUSON, (now living,) fenced in without reference to the streets, which now cut through it. The stubble of that field is still decaying in the soil around the foundations of that noble edifice." In this wheat field, we terminate our wanderings through the Cincinnati of 1800. To the west were mere woods and paths; to the north, Main street was a muddy country road, which soon divided into two,—one winding over the hills to Dayton, the other, as now, passing through the valley of Millcreek, to Hamilton.

On the 4th of July, 1799, the guns of Fort Washington, at morning dawn, poured forth a salute to the last National Anniversary of the 18th century. The troops and militia paraded under Governer ST. CLAIR, and joy, festivities, and sports crowned the day. The Indian conquest was terminated; Fort Washington ceased to be of consequence; the pioneer village began to be a town; and Cincinnati, the Metropolis of the West, began its career of civil and commercial prosperity.

In the fifty years which have intervened between the village and the present city, there were few events which were not in the natural progress of rapid growth, or common to the commercial vicissitudes of the country. There were, however, a few

FIRST PRESBYTERIAN CHURCH, (NEW EDIFICE,) ERECTED 1851-2.

which were peculiar, in their character, to the natural history of this region, and have become memorable in the annals of the city. The first of these were the EARTHQUAKES of 1811-12. These came upon the inhabitants with great surprise. There were no volcanic mountains within many hundreds of miles, and no such phenomena were known to the early settlers. On the morning of the 16th of December, 1811, the inhabitants of Cincinnati, and the neighborhood, were roused from their beds by a severe shock of earthquake, lasting six or seven minutes, the vibrations of which were from the South West to the North East. On the 23d of January, 1812, was another shock, and on the 7th of February, another, harder than either. In the meanwhile, scarcely a day elapsed without evident shaking of the earth. It was ascertained, by an instrument prepared for the purpose, that from December to May there was not a day without vibrations. Agitations were felt at subsequent periods, for more than a year, but they gradually wore off, and with the exception of two or three very slight vibrations, have not returned since. The original seat of these earthquakes was near New Madrid, (Mo.) on the Mississippi, where it changed the course of the river, and converted the solid land into pools and lakes.

Some of the shocks at Cincinnati were so violent as to shake down chimneys and partition walls! In WILLIS' Tavern, on Main street, many of the young gentlemen and ladies of the town were boarders. When the first shock came, they rushed into the street as if the Judgment had come, and many a humorous story was told at the time,—of mamas in their night caps, of papas in their drawers, of maiden beauty unadorned, of bold and slashing soldiers pale with fear,—as the motley group of old and young were exhibited flying from their beds in the light of a December moon!

In May, 1809, there came through this region, one of those tornadoes, which in those days were more common than they are now, and were often extremely violent. This wind, like nearly all storms in this valley, commenced in the South West, and by half-past 1, P. M. of the 28th, became a whirlwind of prodigious force,—sweeping principally over the eastern part of the town. The roof of the "Sargent House," as it was called,

3

standing alone, where Macalister street now is,—was blown off like a sheet of paper, and carried to the plain below! A new brick school house was blown down; while fences, trees, etc. were uprooted and scattered about in every direction. As the tornado proceeded eastwardly, it made a clear track through the forest, prostrating at once the largest oaks. The road through Lebanon and Wilmington was in many places impassable on account of the labyrinth of trees thrown across it by the tempest, This storm ascended the slope of the Alleghanies, in the afternoon, and, in a few hours more, passed away to the ocean.

Another memorable event was the "FLOOD" of 1832. There have been other "freshets" of the Ohio, as high, or nearly so, as this; but none which which was so injurious, or remarkable in its effects. An Indian tradition told of yet higher waters, just previous to the arrival of the whites; and in December, 1847, another occurred, within a few inches of the same height. In 1832, however, far more damage was done. The water began to be high on the 7th of February, and continued rapidly rising till the 19th, when it had attained the extraordinary height of sixty-three feet above low water mark! Many frame houses on the banks of the river were floated off, and seen hundreds of miles from the place where built, on the way to the Mississippi. Boats were unmoored, men were drowned, animals were destroyed, steamers floated over fields of corn, and run foul of the forest trees. The river Ohio from the surrounding heights, was as if an ocean had broken over the country, and threatened all the abodes of man. That part of the city near the mouth of Mill Creek, was all submerged; the roofs only of the smaller houses were to be seen, and the taller ones stood like islands in the deep. Steamboats passed up Main to Second street, and the great warehouses on the bottom could be reached only in boats.

This extraordinary "flood" is said to have been caused by the concurrence of three facts, which can rarely happen at the same time. In the first place, the ground was frozen, so that the water could not be absorbed by the earth; then the heavy snows of the mountains melted; and lastly, an immense quantity of rain fell at the same time. A vast amount of water thus accumulated, which instead of sinking into the earth, was rolled off into the Ohio, and its tributaries. The ordinary spring floods of the Ohio, do not reach any part of Cincinnati; and it is only once in about twenty years, that these great floods may be anticipated.

The next remarkable event in the history of Cincinnati, was the invasion of the CHOLERA. This was indeed common to nearly all the cities and towns of the country, but there were few which have been visited so severely, or so frequently. The severity of this epidemic here, serves to prove how great and permanent are those causes of growth and prosperity, which have been able not only to overcome such disasters, but in a very brief period to wipe away all traces of their existence. The first visit of the Cholera, was in September, 1832, and continued till the 1st of December following; its greatest violence being in October. In 1833 it returned with less force, and again in the summer of 1834. In these three seasons, about 1500 persons perished with that disease, the population being about 30,000; the mortality by cholera was 1 in 20. In 1849, seventeen years after its first invasion, this destroyer returned again, and with great violence; its prevalence in that season, was chiefly among the foreign immigrants; the Germans and Irish. In 1850, it again returned, and in 1851, slightly, making in all six years, since 1832, in which the cholera has been present. In the three last seasons, about 7000 died of cholera, making a little more than 1 in 20, or very near the same ratio as before. With the exception of cholera which has pervaded all countries, and in some much more fatally, Cincinnati has been remarkably healthy, having, strictly speaking, no epidemic of any kind; fever is not common, and consumption not so frequent as in the Eastern States.

The earthquake, the tornado, the flood, the cholera, were all but temporary disturbances in the course of nature. The first occurred but once in half a century, the second but twice, and the two last appear but casual visitations of Providence. In the meanwhile the village has grown into a town; the town into a city with a suddenness, a power, and a prosperity, which have no precedent, even in this prosperous country.

THE LICKING RIVER—we have spoken of as the war path of the Shawanese. This stream has been remarkable for as many Indian battles, and scenes of danger and adventure as any other locality in the Ohio Valley. DANIEL BOONE, the first settler of

Kentucky, was the first white man whose enterprise has signalized the Licking in history. It was in February, 1778, while engaged with a party in making salt, that the bold pioneer was captured by the Indians. They took him to Old Chil-li-cothe, on the Little Miami, just above the present Xenia, thence they took him to Detroit, with a view of selling him (for ransom) to the English; but his captors finally concluded to keep him, his virtues having fairly gained their affections. The following account of BOONE and his escape is given in the "Western Annals:"

"No man could have been better calculated than BOONE to disarm the suspicions of the red men. Some have called him a white Indian, and, except that he never showed the Indian's blood-thirstiness when excited, he was more akin in his loves, his ways, his instincts, his joys, and his sorrows to the aboriginal inhabitants of the West, than to the Anglo-Saxon invaders. Scarce any other white possessed in any equal degree the true Indian gravity, which comes neither from thought, feeling, or vacuity, but from a bump peculiar to their own craniums. And so in hunting, shooting, and swimming, and other Shawanese amusements, the newly made Indian boy Boone spent the month of May, necessity making all the little inconveniences of his lot quite endurable.

"On the first of June, his aid was required in the business of salt-making, and for that purpose he and his brethren started for the valley of the Scioto, where he stayed ten days, hunting, boiling brine, and cooking; then the homeward path was taken again. But when Chillicothe was once more reached, a sad sight met our friend Daniel's eyes; four hundred and fifty of the choice warriors of the West, painted in the most exquisite war style, and armed for the battle. He scarce needed to ask whither they were bound; his heart told him Boonesborough; and already, in imagination, he saw the blazing roofs of the little borough he had founded; and he saw the bleeding forms of his friends. Could he do nothing? He would see; meanwhile be a good Indian, and look all ease and joy. He was a long way from his own white homestead; one hundred and fifty miles at least, and a rough and inhospitable country much of the way between him and it. But he had travelled fast and far, and might again. So, without a word to his fellow prisoners, early in the morning of June 16th, without his breakfast, in the most secret manner, unseen, unheard, he departed. He left his red relatives to mourn his loss, and over hill and valley sped, forty miles a day, for four successive days, and ate but one meal by the way. He found the station wholly unprepared to resist so formidable body as that which threatened it, and it was a matter of life and death that every muscle should be exerted to get all in readiness for the expected visitors. Rapidly the white men toiled in the summer sun, and through the summer night, to repair and complete the fortifications, and to have all as experience had shown it should be. But still the foe came not, and in a few days another escaped captive brought information of the delay of the expedition in consequence of BOONE's flight. The savages had relied on surprising the stations, and their plans being foiled by their adopted son Daniel, all their plans were unsettled. Thus it proved the salvation of Boonesborough, and probably of all the frontier forts, that the founder of Kentucky was taken captive and remained a captive as long as he did. So often do seeming misfortunes prove, in God's hand, our truest good."

In 1779, an expedition was made by the Licking, to the Indian towns, which failed; and in 1779, a body of 600 Canadians and Indians made an expedition up the Licking. It was in consequence of repeated incursions on the settlements of the Licking, that CLARK made that successful attack on the Indian towns of the Miamis, which for a time relieved Kentucky.

"An expedition which had been in the neighborhood of Lexington, where the first permanent improvements were made in April of this year, (1779,) upon its return came to the Ohio near the Licking, at the very time that Colonel ROGERS and Captain BENHAM reached the same point on their way up the river in boats. A few of the Indians were seen by the commander of the little American squadron, near the mouth of the Licking; and supposing himself to be far superior in numbers, he caused seventy of his men to land, intending to surround the savages; in a few moments, however, he found he was himself surrounded, and after a hard fought battle, only twenty or twenty-five, or perhaps even fewer, of the party were left alive. It was in connection with this skirmish that a coincidence occurred which seems to belong rather to a fanciful story than to sober history, and which yet appears to be well authenticated. In the party of whites was Captain ROBERT BENHAM. He was one of those that fell, being shot through both hips, so as to be powerless in his lower limbs; he dragged himself, however, to a tree-top, and there lay concealed from the savages after the contest was over. On the evening of the second day, seeing a raccoon, he shot it, but no sooner was the crack of his rifle heard than he distinguished a human voice, not far distant; supposing it to be some Indian, he re-loaded his gun and prepared for defence; but a few moments undeceived him, and he discovered that the person whose voice he had heard was a fellow sufferer, with this difference, however, that both his arms were broken! Here then, were the only two survivors of the combat, (except those who had entirely escaped,) with one pair of legs and one pair of arms between them. It will be easily believed that they formed a co-partnership for mutual aid and defence. BENHAM shot the game which his friend drove towards him, and the man with sound legs then kicked it to the spot where he with sound arms sat ready to cook it. To procure water, the one with legs took a hat by the brim in his teeth, and walked into the Licking up to his neck, while the man with arms was to make signals if any boat appeared in sight. In this way they spent about six weeks, when, upon the 27th of November, they were rescued. BENHAM afterward bought and lived upon the land where the battle took place; his companion, Mr. BUTLER tells us, was, a few years since, still living at Brownsville, Pennsylvania."

CLARK was a remarkable man, whose memory is yet renowned in the West. His knowledge of Indian character was perfect, while his self-command and courage were unrivalled. The following scene, characteristic of the man, is said to have taken place, at Fort Finney, mouth of the Great Miami, and is from a late work, by Judge HALL:

"The Indians entered in a disorderly and disrespectful manner; the commissioners without noticing the disorderly conduct of the other party, or appearing to have discovered their meditated treachery, opened the council in due form. They lighted the peace-pipe, and after drawing a few whiffs, passed it to the chiefs who received it. Colonel CLARK then rose to explain the purpose for which the treaty was ordered. With an unembarrassed air, with the tone of one accustomed to command, and an easy assurance of perfect security and self possession, he stated that the commissioners had been sent to offer peace to the Shawanese; that the President had no wish to continue the war; he had no resentment to gratify; and if the red men desired peace, they could have it on reasonable terms. 'If such be the will of the Shawanese,' he concluded, 'let some of their wise men speak.'

"A chief arose, drew up his tall person to its full height, and assuming a haughty attitude, threw his eye contemptuously over the commissioners and their small retinue, as if to measure their insignificance, in comparison with his own numerous train, and then stalking to the table, threw upon it two belts of wampum, of different colors—the war and the peace belt.

"'We come here,' he exclaimed, 'to offer you two pieces of wampum; they are of different colors; you know what they mean: you can take which you like!' and turning upon his heel, he resumed his seat.

"The chiefs drew themselves up, in the consciousness of having hurled defiance in the teeth of the white men. They offered an insult to the renowned leader of the Long Knives, to which they knew it would be hard to submit, while they did not suppose he dare resent it. The council-pipe was laid aside. those fierce wild men gazed intently at CLARK. The Americans saw that the crisis had arrived; they could no longer doubt that the Indians understood the advantage they possessed, and were disposed to use it; and a common sense of danger caused each eye to be turned on the leading commissioner. He sat undisturbed and apparently careless until the chief who had thrown the belts upon the table had taken his seat; then with a small cane which he held in his hand, he reached, as if playfully, towards the war belt, entangled the end of the stick in it, drew it towards him, and then with a switch of the cane threw the belt into the midst of the chiefs. The effect was electric. Every man in the council, of each party, sprang to his feet,—the savage with a loud exclamation, 'Hugh!'—the Americans in expectation of a hopeless conflict against overwhelming numbers.—Every hand grasped a weapon.

"CLARK alone was unawed. The expression of his countenance changed to a ferocious sternness and his eye flashed, but otherwise he was unmoved. A bitter smile was perceptible upon his compressed lips, as he gazed upon that savage band, whose hundred eyes were bent fiercely and in horrid exultation upon him as they stood like a pack of wolves at bay thirsting for blood, and ready to rush upon him whenever one bolder than the rest should commence the attack. It was one of those moments of indecision when the slightest weight thrown into either scale will make it preponderate; a moment in which a bold man, conversant with the secret springs of human action, may seize upon the minds of all around him and sway them at his will.

"Such a man was the intrepid Virginian. He spoke and there was no man bold enough to gainsay him,—none that could return the fierce glance of his eye. Raising his arm and waiving his hand toward the door, he exclaimed: 'DOGS! YOU MAY GO!' The Indians hesitated for a moment, and then rushed tumultuously out of the council room."*

The stranger, who in this sketch we supposed to be looking upon the Cincinnati of 1800, clustered round Fort Washington, and half hid amidst the thick forests of the Miamis,—now looks upon the busy, active, populous, animated, QUEEN OF THE WEST, resting upon the bosom of the Ohio, spreading out over hill and plain, absorbing the commerce of millions, erecting the laboratories of art, and connecting herself by these rail-cars, with distant States, and attracting the inhabitants of distant lands! Let us suppose this stranger to have actually seen, (as some now living have done,) the *village* of Cincinnati, and returning after half a century, to behold it now. On yonder hill, where WHITE EYES watched from his tree top the soldiers of Fort Washington, rises the OBSERVATORY, having one of the finest Telescopes in the world,—standing, in fact, as the "Light House of the Skies." Where the "corn field" was, on Broadway, rise the splendid mansions of taste and wealth. Where the "wheat field" was, on Sixth street, is the Mechanics' Institute, dedicated to knowledge and science; where the village school house was, rises the massy structure which contains the Mercantile Library and the Merchants' Exchange; where the "ponds" were, on the bottom, are long ranges of stores, and factories, and founderies. All around are thronged streets, and the loud

* HALL, in Wiley & Putnam's Library.

VIEW OF CINCINNATI IN THE YEAR 1809.

roar of business. The slow and narrow "ark" has been supplanted on the water by the swift and splendid steamer; the wagon, by the coach; the mud road, by the railway; and in one word, the forest gloom, the wigwam, and the cabin, have, in a few short years, disappeared before the advancing light of a gorgeous and brilliant civilization, soon to be exhibited in yet more striking manifestations.

The traveller may feel curious to know something of the actual *progress* of Cincinnati, and something of the most interesting *facts* in its present condition. Of these we can give only a bird's eye view, and that in the dry form of statistics, and statements. The growth of Cincinnati for the last half century, and its *rate* of increase is denoted in the following table:

TABLE OF THE POPULATION AND GROWTH OF CINCINNATI WITHIN THE CORPORATE LIMITS

Years.	Population.	Decennial Increase.	Per Cent.
1800	500		
1810	2,320	1,820	360
1820	9,602	7,282	314
1830	24,831	15,229	158
1840	46,338	21,507	87
1850	116,108	69,770	150

Calculating the growth of Cincinnati, both on its *increments* and also its *per centage* of increase, the result will give 236,000 for the population in 1860, and make it the *third* city of the American Union. Looking to all the elements of progress now at work to increase its business and add to its attraction, this estimate is not extravagant.

To the above table of population, we add one of the growth of the northern suburbs, or what were the northern suburbs in 1840. Since then, what are now denominated the 11th and 12th Wards, have been cut off from Millcreek Township. The comparison of population in the suburbs is as follows, viz:

	In 1840.	In 1850.
Mill Creek Township, - - - -	6,249	6,287
Eleventh Ward, - - - - - -		} 19,336
Twelfth Ward, - - - - - -		
Total, - - - - -	6,249	25,623

This suburb has therefore increased at the rate of 300 per cent, and, at this rate, there will be in 1860, nearly 100,000 inhabitants north of the city line in 1840! A general idea of the business of Cincinnati may be obtained from the following statistics:

1. VALUE OF MANUFACTURED ARTICLES and Industrial production, - - - - - - - - - $55,017,000

2. EXPORTS of strictly Domestic Produce, - - $10,000,000
of Southern Productions, - - - 4,500,000
of Merchandise and Manufactures, 36,500,000

Total, - - - - - - $51,000,000

3. THE IMPORTS may be taken, as in general, equal to the exports, or at least but little less.

THE TRADE of Cincinnati may be estimated, in the aggregate, as nearly or quite equal to one hundred millions of dollars.

As an example of the manufacturing industry of this western city, take the following values of some of the leading articles manufactured for general distribution, and not including any of those, such as carpentry, brick-laying, baking, etc., which are only local.

MANUFACTURE OF		
	IRON, of all varieties,	$5,547,900
	CLOTH AND CLOTHING,	4,427,500
	LEATHER,	2,589,650
	WOOD AND FURNITURE,	2,356,890
	GREASE AND OILS,	4,545,000
	ALCOHOL AND LIQUORS,	4,191,920
	COPPER AND TIN,	515,000
	ANIMAL MEATS,	5,895,000
	BOOKS AND PUBLICATIONS,	1,246,540
	CARS AND CARRIAGES,	355,937
	CHEMICALS,	226,000
	FLOUR AND FEED,	1,690,000
	TOBACCO,	931,000
	STEAMBOATS,	488,000
	WHITE LEAD,	385,000
	MISCELLANEOUS,	458,000
	Total,	$35,849,337

These, as the list shows, do not include the value of merely mechanical labor employed in the city.

4. CHURCHES AND RELIGIOUS ESTABLISHMENTS.—About *one-third* of the inhabitants of Cincinnati are Roman Catholics, who have come from Europe, immigrants in this country. Of these, two-thirds are Germans, who have brought their religion and their language with them. Another large body of Germans are Lutherans, more than one-half of whom are Rationalists. *Six* German Lutheran churches are of this description. The Irish are nearly all Roman Catholics. The Welsh (of whom there are three churches,) are Presbyterians and Methodists. The American churches are divided among the usual Protestant denominations. The following table shows the number of churches in each sect, viz:

EPISCOPALIAN, - - - -	5,	ROMAN CATHOLIC, - -	11,
PRESBYTERIAN, (all kinds,)	19,	METHODISTS, (all kinds,)	22,
BAPTISTS, (all kinds,) -	12,	LUTHERAN, (all kinds,)	10,
FRIENDS, - - - - -	2,	GERMAN REFORMED, -	2,
SWEDENBORGIANS, - -	2,	UNITARIANS, - - -	2,
UNIVERSALISTS, - -	2,	UNITED BRETHREN, -	1,
HEBREW SYNAGOGUES, -	4,	SECOND ADVENT, - -	1,

At the present time, the whole number of churches and religious institutions exceeds 100. The proportion between the great divisions of religious persuasion is estimated thus: Protestants, 62 per cent; Roman Catholics, 35 per cent; and Jews, 3 per cent. The number of foreign immigrants is 46 per cent. and of Americans 54 per cent. It follows from these two statements compared, that 8 per cent of the population are *foreign Protestants,* and that the *foreign* Catholics are to the *foreign* Protestants as 35 to 8, and 3 per cent are Jews. Of all the foreign immigrants, therefore, just *three-fourths* are Roman Catholics.

SCHOOLS AND EDUCATION.—Cincinnati has had a high reputation for its elementary schools; so much so that many families have removed to the city from interior counties, solely to enjoy the benefits of the public schools. These schools are *free* and give a good *common education.* There are also many excellent private institutions, and the Roman Catholic churches have a system of parochial schools. In addition to this there are Female Schools, Academies, and Colleges; besides, Commercial Institutes, Orphan Asylums, Libraries, Medical Colleges, Law

Schools, etc. On the whole, there is scarcely any species of instruction which may not be enjoyed at Cincinnati, and at a cheap rate. Cheap boarding for students may also be had, and there are great facilities for the pursuit of education, both for strangers and citizens.

The statistics of Schools, Academies, and Colleges, etc. in Cincinnati, are as follows:

Institutions.	Number.	Teachers.	Pupils.
Public Schools,	19	138	12,240
Parochial Schools,	13	48	4,494
Private Schools,	50	100	2,500
Colleges,	3	15	403
Medical Colleges,	4	20	450
Mercantile Colleges,	4	12	250
Law School,	1	3	40
Theological Schools,	5	7	100
Colored Schools,	3	9	360
Totals,	102	352	20,837

More than twenty thousand youth are there annually instructed in Cincinnati, in various branches of education, and as the time usually allotted to elementary education is much less than that within which the law limits public education, in that period there is a succession of pupils. It is probable that nearly all the youth of Cincinnati are more or less taught in its schools.

Commercial Institutions.—Banks, Insurance Offices, Private Bankers, the Merchants' Exchange, the Mercantile Library Association, Commercial Colleges, and all the associations for the convenience and promotion of commercial interests, which are found in any city, exist also in Cincinnati. The city has been, and is yet deficient in banking capital, in proportion to the wants of trade. As a consequence, money is in active demand, and the rate of interest high. The disadvantage to the commerce of the city is great, but the profits of business, the sale of domestic products, and the flourishing condition of manufactures, have rapidly accumulated the wealth of the city, and there is among the citizens a large class of wealthy men. The value of property exceeds sixty millions of dollars, and the annual accumulation is at least a tenth part of that. Should its present prosperity continue, the wealth of Cincinnati will, in a few years, equal that of New York.

PUBLIC AND CHARITABLE INSTITUTIONS.—A portion of these we have already mentioned. There are others of a protective and charitable nature, in which a stranger will feel interested.

THE HOUSE OF REFUGE is one of these. This is about two miles out of the city, and is an institution for the reclamation of youth, of both sexes, who are either viciously inclined, have committed small crimes, or are in dangerous ways, without friends. It is an interesting place, and worth a visit.

THE COMMERCIAL HOSPITAL, was originally intended for boatmen, for whom an allowance is made by Government; but has gradually become a depository of all the sick poor, who, having no other shelter, are here cared for by the Township Trustees. In consequence of the deficiency of Lunatic Asylums, about 120 lunatics are annually maintained in the Hospital. Women, also, are taken there to lie-in. Patients of all other kinds are also taken there, especially strangers. More than three thousand persons are provided for annually, in this institution.

THE WIDOW'S HOME, on Mount Auburn, is a new charity instituted originally as a home for respectable and aged females. The building has just been erected, and it promises to be useful and beneficent.

The ORPHAN ASYLUMS are five in number and contain four hundred inmates. One is American Protestant, one German Protestant, one Colored, and two Roman Catholic.

The HOTEL FOR INVALIDS is a private institution for the reception of patients, who having no home, and unwilling to go to the hospital, may here have comfortable attendance and physicians, in comparative retirement.

TEMPERANCE, MASONIC, AND ODD-FELLOWS Societies are numerous, and have large halls in different parts of the city.

A stranger, who visits Cincinnati, may, if he pleases, find much to interest and occupy him. If he desires to read in quiet and comfort, few places in the United States afford a better selection of either books or newspapers, than may be found in the beautiful library room of the Mercantile Library Association, Walnut, between Fourth and Fifth streets. If he loves the Fine Arts, the Galleries of Paintings, of which there are two, will amuse him for a few hours, and he may also step into the studios of several who are no mean Artists. If he loves Music, there is scarcely an evening without a concert. If he would attend church, there are those of all denominations, who will make him welcome to a seat. Finally, if he be a lover of scenery, and the beauties of nature, he has only to walk or ride over the neighboring hills to behold the most charming views, and delight his eye with the most varied landscapes. From Mount Adams, where the Observatory stands sentinel of the skies; or Mount Auburn, where picturesque gardens and sloping hills are all around, or on the Vine street summits; or over the hills of Mill-creek; or of Kentucky, beyond the river; every where, and all around, the environs of Cincinnati are filled with beautiful and picturesque scenes. In this respect, there is scarcely a town in the United States which equals it. The graceful curves of the surrounding hills, and the gentle windings of the Ohio have supplied the elements of great loveliness in scenery. Travelers from Europe and America have been alike delighted with the aspects of Nature and Art, presented by the environs of Cincinnati. The stranger, who remains more than a day, will scarcely be just to himself who does not take an opportunity to ride over the hills and villages which surround the plain of the city.

St. Peter's Cathedral, on Plum street, between Seventh and Eighth streets, is one of the most beautiful and imposing buildings in the Western country. It is built in the most chaste style of Grecian architecture. Its lofty spire rises 275 feet in height, and its base is a fine portico and colonade. In the rear is the home of Archbishop Purcell and his subordinate Priests. It is built of gray limestone, and has an appearance of both solidity and grandeur.

Having now dwelt for a time on the village of 1800, as well as the city of the present, and glanced at some of its events, its history, and reminiscences, we must bid farewell to the Queen of the West, and hasten with our traveler up the Valley of the Miami.

Cincinnati, Hamilton, and Dayton Railway.—Before we commence our journey, let us take a bird's eye glance at the road we are about to travel on. Dayton is a large and flourishing town on the Great Miami river, sixty miles from Cincinnati, whence many roads diverge in various directions, and which is the southern terminus of the Mad River and Sandusky Railroad—of the Western Railroad from Greenville—of the Dayton, Troy

ST. PETER'S CATHEDRAL.

and Michigan Railroad—and consequently of a large trade and extensive connections. This railway connects Dayton with Cincinnati, by way of Hamilton, also a large and flourishing town on the Great Miami.

The work was commenced December, 1849, and finished September, 1851, being much of the time interrupted by the cholera in 1850. Its length is 59 80-100 miles, of which 45 30-100 miles are straight line, and 14 50-100 miles curved. The total ascent from Cincinnati to Dayton is 241 3-10 feet, being composed of 361 3-10 feet ascending grades northwardly, and 110 feet southwardly. Of these grades, only one-eighth part are over ten feet to a mile, and there are no high grades on the line.

We shall soon see, that the work is well constructed, solid, and substantial.

The Station House of the Hamilton and Dayton Railway.—We are now about starting from the handsome and spacious station house on Sixth street. The steam is whizzing in our ears and the passengers are getting impatient. Some are buying newspapers, some oranges, some a book; some are just arriving in omnibuses; trunks are tumbling into the baggage-car, and friends are parting. "Where is my trunk?—give me the check." "Have you got my carpet-bag?"—"All right, sir!" The hackmen and draymen are quarreling. Every passenger knows the train will start precisely at the time; yet everybody is nervous, and looking at their watches, except two or three old stagers, who are quietly looking on the scene. There goes the whistle! But, stop--we must look a moment at this Station House. It is a solid, ample building, well adapted to the purpose, 500 feet in length and 103 feet in breadth—two stories high on each front, with offices and commission rooms above. It was built on ground bought of Mr. HATHAWAY, one of the oldest and richest citizens of Cincinnati. The history of this ground will illustrate one of the most striking features of Cincinnati—the rapid rise in the value of real estate. It is a good test of the prosperity and general growth of the town. In November, 1811, Mr. HATHAWAY bought of Col. BARR, who then owned a farm comprising the western part of Cincinnati, 101 22-100 acres, for $1,122, being about $11 per acre! This property is probably worth now a million of dollars, or from $20 to $100 per front foot, according to situation. The increased value of the whole is 1000 per cent! Two or three other examples will probably give the stranger a more vivid idea of the same fact. Judge BURNET lives on the north-west corner of Seventh and Elm streets—now near the center of the town. In 1803, he bought about seven acres, on that and the adjoining square, for $750. This is now worth, if the improvements were off, at least 30,000 per cent. in advance. On part of this property the Roman Catholic Cathedral is built, and on another, St. John's (Episcopal) Church. Take an example in another part of the town. In 1807, the Reservation around Fort Washington was sold at public sale. The lot, at the south-east corner of Fourth and Broadway, (45½ feet by 100), was sold for $137 50-100, or, about $3 per foot. It is now worth $350 per foot, or 10,000 per cent. advance! An examination of these rates proves, that property in the most populous parts of the city, has doubled in value each six years for half a century. In the out-lots, it has doubled in less time. Below where the Station House now is, and between the then town (east of Walnut street) and Mill-creek, lies what in old times was called "Hobson's Choice," being the encampment of WAYNE's Army, in 1793. It was so called, because it was the only suitable place to be found. Here WAYNE drilled his troops for the ensuing campaign. On the Fifth street Mound, to which we have before alluded, he planted a sentry, having cut off the apex. In the fall of 1793, he marched into what is now Darke county, and built Fort Greenville, where the town of Greenville now is. In July, 1794, he left there, and on the 20th of August, defeated the Indians, in the battle of the "Fallen Timbers," Lucas county.

In passing from the Station to Mill-creek bottom, we see low ground to the right and left.

It was near this spot, on the 7th October, 1790, that the following incident and battle took place, which is designated by the early settlers as the Legend of Jacob Wetzel:

A Legend of Jacob Wetzel.—The road along the Ohio river leading to Storrs and Delhi, some four hundred yards below the junction of Front and Fifth streets, crosses what, in early days, was the outlet of a water-course, and notwithstanding the changes made by the lapse of years, and the building improvements adjacent, the spot still possesses many features of its original surface, although now divested of its forest character. At the period of this adventure—October 7, 1790—besides the dense forest of maple and beech, its heavy undergrowth of spice-wood and grape-vine made it an admirable lurking place for the savage beasts, and more savage still, the red men of the woods.

Wetzel had been out on his accustomed pursuit—hunting—and was returning to town, at that time a few cabins and huts collected in the space fronting the river, and extending from Main street to Broadway. He had been very successful, and was returning to procure a horse to bear a load too heavy for his own shoulders, and, at the spot alluded to, had sat down on a decaying tree-trunk to rest himself, and wipe the sweat from his brow, which his forcing his way through the brush had started, cool as was the weather, when he heard the rustling of leaves and branches, which betokened that an animal or an enemy was approaching. Silencing the growl of his dog, who sat at his feet, and appeared equally conscious of danger, he sprang behind a tree and discovered the dark form of an Indian, half hidden by the body of a large oak, who had his rifle in his hands, ready for any emergency that might require the use of it, as he, too, appeared to be on his guard, having heard the low growling of the dog. At this instant, the dog also spied the Indian and barked aloud, which told the Indian of the proximity of his enemy. To raise his rifle was but the work of a moment, and the distinct cracks of two weapons were heard almost at the same time. The Indian's fell from his hands, as the ball of the hunter's had penetrated and broken the elbow of his left arm, while the hunter escaped unhurt. Before the Indian could possibly reload his rifle in his wounded condition, WETZEL had rushed swiftly upon him with his knife, but not before the Indian had drawn his. The first thrust was parried off by the Indian, with the greatest skill, and the shock was so great in the effort that the hunter's weapon was thrown some thirty feet from him. Nothing daunted, he threw himself upon the Indian with all his force and seized him around the body; at the same time encircling the right arm in which the Indian still grasped his knife. The Indian, however, was a very muscular fellow, and the conflict now seemed doubtful indeed. The savage was striving with all his might to release his arm, in order to use his knife. In their struggle, their feet became interlocked, and they both fell to the ground, the Indian uppermost, which extricated the Indian's arm from the iron grasp of the hunter. He was making his greatest endeavors to use his knife, but could not, from the position in which they were lying, as WETZEL soon forced him over on his right side, and consequently he could have no use of his arm.

Just at this point of the deadly conflict, the Indian gave an appalling yell, and, with renewed strength, placed his enemy underneath him again, and with a most exulting cry of victory, as he sat upon his body, raised his arm for that fatal plunge. WETZEL saw death before his eyes, and gave himself up for lost, when, just at this most critical juncture, his faithful dog, who had not been an uninterested observer of the scene, sprang forward, and seized the Indian with such force by the throat, as caused the weapon to fall harmless from his hand. WETZEL, seeing such a sudden change in his fate, made one last and desperate effort for his life, and threw the Indian from him. Before the prostrate savage had time to recover himself, the hunter had seized the knife, and with redoubled energy rushed upon him, and with his foot firmly planted on the Indian's breast, plunged the weapon up to the hilt in his heart. The savage gave one convulsive shudder, and was no more.

As soon as WETZEL had possessed himself of his rifle, together with the Indian's weapons, he started immediately on his way. He had gone but a short distance when his ears were assailed by the startling whoop of a number of Indians. He ran eagerly for the river, and, fortunately finding a canoe on the beach near the water, was soon out of reach, and made his way, without further danger, to the cove at the foot of Sycamore street.

The Indians came up to the place of the recent renconter, and discovered the body of a fallen comrade. They gave a most hideous yell, when, upon examination, they recognized in the dead Indian, the features of one of their bravest chiefs.

The low ground between the track, Mill-creek, and the city, is yet subject to overflow—the Ohio river, in high stage, covering the same to the depth of thirty or forty feet, and the water running back into the interior of this bottom as far as Spring Grove Cemetery. Many projects are on foot to make these low grounds available—of these we may enumerate that of making a large Steamboat Dock, and another to straighten the course of the creek, wall up and fill from the adjacent hill side. Though the present appearance of the ground looks so discouraging for immediate use, still it must be remembered that it is not much more so than was all the low ground immediately below, and parallel to, Third street, and where HARMAR's army only found "Hobson's Choice" to encamp on. And this low ground has been filled up and covered over with manufactories and other substantial improvements, and its former condition is forgotten. Looking to this picture of the progress of the city, it will not probably be many years before the ground, now so low and unpromising, will be as well filled up and covered as that parallel to Third street or on the line of Pearl street.

We can stop no longer. There goes the whistle! We are off. The cars are moving fast by houses and streets, obviously in a new part of the city. Now, we are passing over Mill-creek, on a viaduct just above the bridge, and near the Whitewater Canal. This canal passes down the Whitewater valley, in Indiana, crosses the Great Miami, at Cleves, and meets the Ohio, at the celebrated North Bend, where JOHN CLEVES SYMMES, the original proprietor of the Miami country, settled, and where was the residence and is now the tomb of HARRISON. Thence it passes up the Ohio to Cincinnati. The cars, having passed the viaduct, are now turned north, at the foot of the green hills west of Mill-creek. Just beyond is the point where our artist has taken a hurried view of the city. Prominent in the scene is the Station House and one of the City Schools. The town lies indistinctly before us, and to the south, over the river, are Newport and Covington. At about two miles beyond this we shall see, at the distance of half a mile to the right, a large stone building, in plain but handsome architectural style. It is the HOUSE OF REFUGE. This institution has but just gone into operation; and is destined to be of great importance in reclaiming the vicious or idle youth of the city. The building is supposed to be better adapted to the purpose than any one in the United States. Six acres of ground are inclosed, with a wall seventeen feet high and 2½ feet thick. Four acres more are to be ornamented with trees and shrubbery, and used as pleasure grounds. The following are the dimensions:

MAIN BUILDING, 276 feet front, 57½ feet wide, 4 stories high,
Two Wings, each, 95 2-3 feet long,
REAR BUILDING, 114 feet long, 56 feet wide, 2 stories high.
WORK ROOM, 40 feet long, 1 story.

There are over 250 rooms, including dormitories, in the building. There are apartments for every use, and conveniences of every description. The material is limestone from the adjoining hills. Cisterns, drains, gas lights, and all the accessories which can make such an establishment comfortable, economical, and useful, are there. It cost about $150,000, and is an honorable testimonial to the public spirit and practical benevolence of Cincinnati.

THE HOUSE OF REFUGE.

CUMMINSVILLE.—We are now approaching the first Station after leaving Cincinnati. Just as we come up, by casting the eye to the right, the rounded slopes of green and pleasant hills are seen beyond Mill-creek. On one of the first of these may be seen a large country house, surrounded by conservatories, shrubbery and fruit trees. This is the residence of R. B. BOWLER, Esq., a merchant of Cincinnati, and is one of a number which make up the beautiful village of CLIFTON. There are few places in the United States, in which so many charms of a quiet, rural, suburban retreat are so united as in this "loveliest village," (not of the *plains*, but of the hills), where

> "Smiling spring its earliest visit paid,
> And parting summer's ling'ring blooms delay'd."

These hills and Cumminsville may be said to terminate Cincinnati. On the hills there will be found some of the most beautiful suburban residences in the vicinity of the city, and the view from them embraces not only the plain below, but a stretch of country, hill and valley, for twenty miles distant. The Corporation of Cincinnati extends over the hill adjoining Clifton, and the streets of the city are rapidly being extended up the ravines and *over* the hills. In Clifton and the surrounding hills, it is supposed, that if Cincinnati increases in population as rapidly as she has for a few years past, many of the best residences of the city will be found. The spire that is seen in Clifton, just beyond Cumminsville, and opposite the Cemetery, is that of the Clifton Church of Bishop McIlvaine, of the Episcopal Church.

A few years since, Clifton was part of the farm of an enterprizing merchant who failed, and transferred it to one of the Banks. It was laid out in small tracts, and soon disposed of, to gentlemen of taste and refinement, who could appreciate the value as well as beauty of such a place. It is now improved in villas, to each of which is attached several acres of ground, laid out in gardens, vineyards, lawns, and walks. In this place, Judge M'Lean, of the Supreme Court, Bishop McIlvaine, Senator Chase, and others known to the public, have their summer residences. Among the earliest settlers was Robert Buchanan, Esq., a merchant, who is distinguished as a Naturalist and a Horticulturist. He is at present one of the cultivators of the Grape, and of the Native Wine. He has over 20,000 grape-bearing vines. This cultivation has increased in the neighborhood of Cincinnati with great rapidity. There are now about *eleven hundred acres of vine-yards* in this vicinity, and it is supposed that the wine produced amounts, in all, to *three hundred thousand gallons*, which may be estimated as worth so many dollars. The banks of the Ohio river are well adapted to the culture of vines, and there is little doubt that this branch of agriculture will increase, until it becomes of great importance. The grape used is almost universally the Catawba. Foreign varieties are found to be much inferior in this climate; and no other native grape is, on the whole, equal to this.

We are now at the Station, (five miles), just *twelve minutes* from the start! How times have changed! It would have taken the early settlers two hours to come this five miles, with mud up to the horses' girths.

Just in front of us, where the weeping willow bends over the fish pond, is the residence of Jacob Hoffner, a retired merchant. The garden and grounds of this house are deemed, in the variety of flowers, plants, shrubs, and trees, one of the finest in our country. The most beautiful and rare plants have been collected, and the grounds arranged with taste and skill. The green houses are kept in fine order, and the products of this garden are among the most interesting to be seen in the annual exhibitions of the Horticultural Society. In 1812, this place was known as "HUTCHINSON'S TAVERN," and in May of that year, the 1st Division of Ohio Militia was paraded back of this house, and volunteers for HULL'S army called for. Nearly every man volunteered, so great was the patriotism of the people at that time. Just about a quarter or third of a mile from this station, is a frame house with wings, known as "LUDLOW STATION." The house is on the left hand (going up) and the cars pass within a few yards of it. This was the residence of Col. ISRAEL LUDLOW, one of the original proprietors of Cincinnati, from 1800 to 1805, and of the Surveyor General of the United States from 1805 to 1809. The term "*Station*" was applied, in those early days, to the houses of some of the principal settlers,—indicating, probably, a place of rendezvous, in case of danger. "LITTLE TURTLE," the wisest and most intelligent chief of the North-Western Indians, commanding them at ST. CLAIR'S defeat, transacted business at the Surveyor General's Office, as late as 1808.

The cars are now passing "SPRING GROVE CEMETERY," where white monuments, scattered amidst green trees, may be seen on the rising ground to your left. This City of the Dead is beautifully laid out—something in the manner of Greenwood, New York. The whole extent of ground, comprising 220 acres—surrounded by a hedge of Osage Orange—is laid off into streets and avenues, and is diversified with hill and dale. About twenty miles of streets and walks are already prepared and in use. The number of lot owners is more than a thousand, and already many beautiful monuments have been erected, which may be seen scattered on the rising ground beyond. In the distant parts of the Cemetery the hills are abrupt, and the vales deep and wooded, which affords an opportunity (well taken advantage of) to vary and diversify the walks, and throw a pleasant air of natural ruralness and simplicity around the scene. Many of the dead which lay in the dust and noise of the city, have been disentombed and laid amidst silent, solemn walks and shades. While the dead lie thick, and thickening with every hour of time, here run the cars, with the vain and ambitious living, concerting new schemes and new works, which scarce all time can perform!

"On this side and on that, men see their friends
Drop off, like leaves in autumn; yet launch out
Into fantastic schemes, which the long livers
In the world's hale and undegen'rate days,
Could scarce have leisure for; ——"

CARTHAGE—ten miles from Cincinnati, fifty miles from Dayton. We stop in the edge of a little wood. The large, fine-looking building to the right, is a Hydropathic establishment. Water is a capital thing; but isn't it queer, we never found out before what a wonderful medicine it is? There was once a great Rain-water Doctor. If he were alive now, he would doubtless find plenty of business; for surely that water which falls from heaven must be the best!

This little wood, on whose edge we stop, has been in times past a famous gathering spot. It was the appointed place for many years of the political meetings of the Whig and Democratic parties. These trees have listened to the voice of many a man whose name is perpetuated in history. Here, thousands were wrapt in wonder at the eloquence of CORWIN, the once "Wagon Boy;" here, JONES, of Tennessee, was heard; here, ALLEN, and here under these trees have sat CLAY, and HARRISON, and JOHNSON, and many another, whose fame has gone through the land. The trees are fast disappearing, like the red Indian, who once gathered here at his Council Fire. Soon the trees will be gone, and the traditions of these scenes, like all the past, will fade dim, and more dimly, on the memory. Perhaps this Railroad Station will remain, and these lines be the only history of what once were moving events and stirring scenes in this land!

LOCKLAND.—This village, quite a thriving one, is scarcely visible from the Railroad. It is situated on the Miami Canal, where there are three locks, affording a large water-power. There are several mills and factories here, which do an extensive business.

POOR HOUSE—twelve miles from Cincinnati. On the left may be seen a large stone building, which is the Cincinnati Poor House. The building and ground have cost $150,000, and there are to be kept, and as far as possible, maintained, by their

own labor, the paupers of Cincinnati. They have heretofore been maintained entirely at the City expense, in the Hospital. It is one of the best plans yet thought of, to transfer the poor of cities to a farm, and work-house, where they can maintain themselves, and will not infect many with the example of idleness, and, too frequently, of vice.

Glendale.—This station is fifteen miles from Cincinnati, and we have reached it in forty minutes. The Railroad here passes through a lovely vale, formerly called "Skillman's Valley." On the left and right are swelling heights, beautifully rounded off. That part of the ground on each side the "Station," especially the ridge on the left, has been bought by a company of thirty gentlemen, and laid out in plats, suitable for country villas. Already we see houses growing up, and soon it will be another Auburn or Clifton, smiling in its rural charms and tasteful improvements, upon the passing stranger. Near this spot, or rather a mile or two beyond, occurred the murder of Col. Elliott, by the Indians. This was rather a notable incident in the early history of the country, and we relate it according to the tradition:

In 1794, Col. Robert Elliott, contractor for supplying the United States army, while traveling with his servant from Fort

Washington to Fort Hamilton, was waylaid and killed by the Indians, at the big hill, south of where THOMAS FLEMING lived, and near the line of Hamilton and Butler counties. When shot, he fell from his horse. The servant made his escape by putting his horse at full speed, followed by that of ELLIOTT's, into Fort Hamilton. The savage who shot the colonel, in haste to take his scalp, drew his knife, and seized him by the wig which he wore. To his astonishment, the scalp came off at the first touch, when he exclaimed, "*dam lie!*" In a few minutes, the surprise of the party was over, and they made themselves merry at the expense of their comrade. The next day, a party from the fort, under the guidance of the servant, visited the spot, placed the body in a coffin and proceeded on their way to Fort Washington. About a mile south of Springdale, they were fired upon by Indians, and the servant, who was on the horse of his late master, was shot at the first fire. The party retreated, leaving the body of ELLIOTT with the savages, who had broken open the coffin, when the former rallied, re-took the body, and carried it, with that of the servant, to Cincinnati, and buried them side by side, in the Presbyterian Cemetery, on Twelfth street."

From Glendale to Hamilton, the cars pass through a farming country, interspersed with wood and field. The distance is ten miles, and is traversed by the Express Train in twenty-eight minutes. There is a station at Jones's, (four miles, which is passed in eight minutes,) but no village.

BUTLER COUNTY LINE—Eighteen miles from Cincinnati, thirty-two from Dayton. We are now entering Butler county, one of the oldest and most fertile counties of the State. We shall traverse it for twenty-five miles; but the following statistical account will give the curious reader more accurate information than he can acquire by the eye only. It is intersected, nearly north and south, by the Great Miami river, which, with its tributaries, Four Mile and Seven Mile creeks on the west, and Gregory's creek on the east, thoroughly water it in every direction, and furnish those rich and broad bottoms on which so much Indian corn is cultivated. It has many thriving towns and villages, of which the principal are Hamilton, Rossville, Middletown, Oxford, Trenton, Monroe, Millville, and Venice.

The following is a tabular view of its population and resources:

Square miles of surface	480	
Population	30,794	
Acres of Land	307,200	
Population to the square mile	65	
Assessed value of Property, Real and Personal	$10,756,633	
Assessed value to each family of 6 Persons	2,100	
Acres of Land in Corn	62,031	
Total Production of Corn	2,646,353	bushels.
Average Production of Corn, per acre	42	"
Acres of Land in Wheat	31,131	
Total Production of Wheat	529,390	bushels.
Average Production of Wheat, per acre	17	"
Number of Cattle in the County	13,044	
" Horses " "	10,175	
" Swine " "	41,515	
" Sheep " "	9,515	

The fertility of Butler county may be known by taking from the above production of corn and wheat an ample amount for the consumption of the people and all the animals, including 20,000 fat hogs, and 4,000 fat cattle. After all that was subtracted, there would remain *one million, three hundred and sixty-five thousand* bushels of corn, and *two hundred and eighty-nine thousand* bushels of wheat surplus for exportation.

HAMILTON AND ROSSVILLE—(25 miles from Cincinnati and 35 from Dayton.)—These make really one town, united by a bridge over the Great Miami river. It is one of the most important country towns in the Miami country, and demands from the passing traveller a few moments' notice. Hamilton is on the Great Miami river, which, flowing from the north, joins the Ohio twenty miles below Cincinnati. The Dayton Railway meets the river at this place, having passed over a gentle and almost imperceptible summit, between the waters of Mill-creek and the Miami. FORT HAMILTON—the origin of the town—was built by the army of ST. CLAIR, in September, 1791. The army, 2,300 strong, marched from Ludlow's Station, before noticed, September 17th, and moved to this point, where they built the Fort, or Stockade, by way of support. It appears from the letters of Captain John Armstrong, employed in its erection, that it was not finished for more than a year. It was completed in the winter of 1792–3. When finally finished, it was quite a respectable fortification, being fifty yards square, with four good bastions, two platforms for cannon, barracks, magazines, officers' quarters, &c. The principal part of this fort was just opposite the east end of the bridge, the southern point extending to the site of the Associate Reformed church. The Mess-room of this fort was the Session-room of the first court held in Butler county, and the Magazine was, as late as 1803, made the county jail. In September, 1793, the army of Wayne encamped on nearly the same ground, in the south part of the present town, on which St. Clair had encamped in 1791. Major Cass, father of the Hon. Lewis Cass, was left in command of Fort Hamilton, while the army moved on to its victory over the Indians.

The town of Hamilton was laid out December 17, 1794, by Israel Ludlow. Rossville, on the west side of the river, was laid out, March 14, 1804, by Mr. John Reilly, agent for the proprietors. These towns grew rather slowly, till within a few years, when the establishment of Hydraulic Works, the construction of the Cincinnati and Dayton Railway, with other improvements, have caused them to grow rapidly in population and importance.

In Hamilton is a monument to John Cleves Symmes, nephew to the founder of the Miami country, and a man signalized by what is called the "Theory of Concentric Spheres"—a very remarkable example of intellectual ingenuity. He had been an officer in the United States Army, and served with distinction, in the war of 1812. In a circular, dated St. Louis, 1818, he first promulgated his theory. He believed, that the earth was composed of concentric spheres; that these were habitable, and that they could be visited through polar openings. This theory he supported with great ingenuity, advancing many facts in evidence of its truth. He delivered lectures on his favorite subject, wrote pamphlets, and petitioned Congress, offering himself to go, on a voyage of discovery, to either Pole. Such a theory, however supported, would naturally meet with little else than ridicule from the world. Congress rejected his petitions, the public laughed, and Captain Symmes lived and died in poverty, leaving behind him not only his theory, but a character amiable, exemplary, and respected. His monument is surmounted with a globe, "open at the Poles."

MIAMI UNIVERSITY is just twelve miles west of Hamilton, in the town of Oxford. This Institution is one of many in the United States, which will stand as monuments to the liberality of the national Government in the cause of education. The township of Oxford was reserved under the contract with Judge SYMMES, for a College. It contains 23,040 acres, which, had it not been permanently leased, at an early day, when prices were low, would now be a most munificent endowment. It has proved, in its present condition, only sufficient to keep up the Institution, without supplying it with such fixtures and libraries as become a University. It is, however, a very useful institution, and has graduated a large number of useful men. It is now under the care of Dr. ANDERSON, and has, in the College Proper, about 120 students.

THE TOWNS of Hamilton and Rossville are now in a state of great prosperity, having the advantage of extensive artificial improvements on every side. The Miami Canal, which was finished more than twenty years since, passes through the town, and affords an opportunity for the concentration and shipment of produce. In the year 1850, there *cleared* from this point on the canal, 102,528 bushels of corn, 18,349 barrels of flour, 1,108,152 pounds of bacon, 1,030,135 lbs. of lard, and 10,025 barrels of pork. All this proves that Hamilton is the center of a very rich agricultural district. Since the canal was built, fine turnpike roads, the Hydraulic Works, and the Hamilton and Dayton Railway have all been constructed.

WATER POWER--HYDRAULIC WORKS.—The water power at this point is equal to that of Lowell, Massachusetts. According to the official estimate and report of SAMUEL FORRER, Esq., Civil Engineer, it is sufficient to propel 166 run of mill stones, allowing 4½ feet of the fall for back-water or rise in the river.

The plan of diverting the Great Miami river from its natural channel and bringing it to Hamilton through an artificial race, was projected by a few citizens of the place in 1842. They procured from the State Legislature a charter for a Joint Stock Company, and pressed forward the work under many embarrassments and difficulties to completion. A dam is constructed across the river about three miles above the town, and about two miles above the crossing of the railroad. The water is conducted through a race seventy feet wide, to a large reservoir, a portion of which may be seen southeast of the railroad bridge above the town. From this reservoir the water is again conducted by a race to the plain of the town, and is distributed in various parts by branch races. The entire fall from the surface of the head race to the surface of the river is 28½ feet; but the natural surface of the ground has enabled the Company so to divide this entire fall, as to provide water for wheels of various dimensions.

The company give perpetual leases of this water-power at the rate of $130 per annum for each mill-stone power—such power being estimated at a certain number of cubic feet per minute over a given fall.

There are now leased and in use, 38 mill-stone powers, and 128 mill-stone powers ready for applicants. On this power at Hamilton, the following establishments are now in successful operation: two large flouring mills, two extensive paper mills, two saw-mills, one planing mill, two iron foundries, one sash factory, two machine-shops, one woollen factory, one plow factory, one sawing establishment and one bedstead factory. Arrangements are in progress for the erection of other establishments of various kinds. This water-power may be said to be the *soul* of Hamilton. One of many facts may be stated to illustrate the value of this water-power to the prosperity of Hamilton. One lot of land was entered on the tax duplicate a few years since, before the work was constructed, at a valuation of $200. The valuation of the same lot with the mills, machinery, and capital now employed on it, is entered on the tax duplicate at one hundred thousand dollars!

Hamilton and Rossville are now supposed to have about 5,000 inhabitants. They are rapidly growing, neatly built, with a public square, on which stand a courthouse and county buildings. They have ten or twelve churches of different denominations, schools, and all the civil and social arrangement of the best country towns. The accompanying view is of Rossville and the Bridge, as seen from below.

The view is taken from the bank of the Miami, on the Rossville side, and shows that part of the town of Rossville, on the turnpike from Indiana to Cincinnati. The bridge is the connection of the towns. The court house in Hamilton is seen beyond the bridge.

THE RAILWAY WAREHOUSE, at Hamilton, is 33 by 240 feet. The cars stop, as is usual in railways, in an unsightly part of the borough;—but, hark!—we are going, whiz!—whiz!—we are passing through the factory suburb, and here is another view looking from the north. Now, we cross the Miami bridge to the west side.

The view on next page is looking towards Hamilton, from the north (upper) side, taken from the Railroad track. The Railroad passes over a part of the old bed of the Miami river. The Mill, Hydraulic Race, a part of the Hydraulic Works, and a portion of Hamilton are seen in this sketch.

THE GREAT MIAMI RIVER—over which we are now passing, is one of the most important streams of the north-west—not for navigation—but in its fertilizing and enriching effects on the country. The entire extent of the valleys of the Great and Little Miamies (only an average distance of twenty miles apart) is 7,500 square miles, and contains a population of 502,000 inhabitants—equal to that of the three States of Vermont, Rhode

6

Island, and Delaware. The Great Miami River is formed by the union of three principal branches. Mad River, whose sources interlock with those of the Scioto—the Miami, which interlocks with the Maumee of the Lakes—and Stillwater, from the north-west. These streams unite at or near Dayton, and give peculiar advantages to that place. We shall now pass up on the west side of the river, and have a full opportunity of seeing the corn-fields, tobacco plantations, and scenery of the Miami Valley.

Eaton and Hamilton Railroad—twenty-five miles from Cincinnati, thirty-five from Dayton. Just over the bridge we have passed, is seen the track of another Railroad diverging to the West. This goes to Eaton, the county seat of Preble county, twenty-five miles, thence to Richmond, the county seat of Wayne county, Indiana, seventeen miles, making forty-two miles from Hamilton, and sixty-nine miles from Cincinnati to Richmond, Indiana. At Richmond it connects with the Indiana Central Railway to Indianapolis, and thence to Terre-Haute and Lafayette, on the Wabash.

Another line, connecting with it, and now constructing, is of great importance. This passes by way of Newcastle and Anderson to Logansport, on the Wabash, and thence to Chicago,

Illinois. From Cincinnati to Richmond is sixty-nine miles; from Richmond to Logansport, 107; from Logansport to Chicago, 113 miles, making 289 miles from Cincinnati to Chicago.

THE VALLEY OF SEVEN MILE CREEK.—The Eaton Railroad takes this valley, and to those who desire an interesting rural trip, this is one of the best routes. This little valley, and indeed the whole country through Preble county, Ohio, and Wayne county, Indiana, is rich and well cultivated.

FOUR MILE VALLEY RAILROAD.—Four Mile Creek joins Seven Mile, near the Great Miami. The Railroad is intended to be made up that stream, a little east of Oxford and Miami University, to Connersville, Indiana. This will be the route from Cincinnati to Oxford.

BUSENBACK'S—30 miles. This is a Station, but, as yet, no town. This, five miles from Hamilton, is run in ten minutes, including the stop. The thirty miles passed from Cincinnati has taken us an hour and eighteen minutes; but we have made *nine stops*, and consumed about twenty-five minutes in that way.

TRENTON—Thirty-three miles from Cincinnati, and twenty-seven from Dayton. This is a small and apparently an old town, on the left. From this point to Dayton the traveller will have a fine opportunity of seeing two species of cultivation, which are the distinguishing features of agriculture in this section—those of Indian Corn and Tobacco. On each side of the way, as the cars pass on, the broad bottoms of the Miami will be seen, extending in an almost perfect level to the foot of the hills. These bottoms are almost inexhaustible in black, rich loam, which has been ages in forming from the decay of immense forests on the spot, mingled with the soil and vegetable matter brought down by the floods in the river. Much of this land has been cultivated for half a century, in Indian Corn, without any change of crops, yet with no exhaustion of its fertility. Of the 62,000 acres of Indian corn cultivated in Butler county, probably one-half of it is in the immediate valley of the Miami. From this point to Dayton, however, much of the valley is cultivated in Tobacco, which is a new crop in this region, but now found very profitable. We shall see more of it in Montgomery county.

MIDDLETOWN.—Thirty-seven miles from Cincinnati, twenty-three miles from Dayton. The Town is on the opposite side of the river, and lies full in view across the broad cornfields which have spread out over the alluvial bottom.

Middletown is a flourishing country village, of about 1,000 inhabitants. It was founded in 1802, and contains three Churches, a Classical Academy, and several stores doing a large business. The town has great advantages from the public works in its neighborhood. The Miami Canal passes through; the Lebanon Canal intersects it here; and now the Railway comes to increase its facilities.

MIDDLETOWN HYDRAULICS.—Two or three miles above Middletown, a dam has been thrown across the Miami, which supplies a great water-power, furnishing business for manufacturing establishments. Within three miles of Middletown, there are eight Grist Mills and a Woollen Factory. A turnpike road crosses the Railway here, which goes from Middletown to West Alexandria, Preble County.

As we pass along the Miami for a few miles, we shall have a fine view of the peculiar features of this section. We shall see nothing abrupt, or rocky, or grand; but everything in scenery is soft, and delicate, and graceful. It is that cast of beauty which

a fertile and exuberant country must ever have. There are no poor lands, nor barren plains, nor mountain cliffs to break the prospect, nor convey the idea of sterility amidst sublime scenes. This soil has no other recommendation than its *fatness*, its perfect capacity to feed the hungry children of men—in one word, to produce peace and plenty! But there are curved heights and wooded summits, and gentle streams around us; all the elements of a calm and benign beauty. Is it not enough?

Post Town—Forty miles from Cincinnati, twenty miles from Dayton. This is only a station, although there appears to be a straggling village in the fields. We are one hour and forty-four minutes from Cincinnati, and fifty minutes from Dayton, according to the Time Table. By the way, this Time Table is an important affair to passengers. What would be the effect o running the train out of time?—only a smash; that is all; but, the traveller may be contented; for experience has proved that railway travelling is by far the safest mode of conveyance.

Carlisle—Forty-four miles from Cincinnati, sixteen miles from Dayton. This is a Station, with some expectation of becoming a town. It is named from George Carlisle, Esq., one of the directors of this Railway Company, and an efficient merchant and banker of Cincinnati.

On the opposite side of the river, and not now in view, is the town of FRANKLIN, one of the thriving villages of the rich county of Warren. Franklin was laid out just after the treaty of Greenville, 1795, by DANIEL C. COOPER and General W. C. SCHENCK, (father of the Hon. R. C. SCHENCK,) two young men, from New Jersey, who built the first cabin near this spot. The town has a Baptist and Methodist, and a Presbyterian church, a high school, several stores, and about 800 inhabitants.

The first vineyard, of any extent, seen on this road, is now in view as presented in this cut, and will show, at a glance, the mode of cultivation most in use, and the manner in which steep, stony, and otherwise useless hill sides are made profitable. We refer to preceding pages for statistics of our wine trade.

MONTGOMERY COUNTY LINE.—We are now at about forty-seven miles from Cincinnati, and thirteen from Dayton, entering the county of Montgomery. This, like the one we have passed through, is a fertile, populous, and wealthy county—the seventh in numbers of the State. The general characteristics of soil and topography are the same as those of the county of Butler, but, as a whole, it is more level and better cultivated. The rural scenery from this to Springfield, Clark county, is eminently pleasing, cheerful, and attractive. It is that of a gently rolling country, watered by clear streams, with large towns in its midst, fine farms, and having all the marks of thrift, comfort, and wealth. This county was originally settled by Jerseymen, as was the whole Miami country—Judge SYMMES, the Patentee, and his friends being from New Jersey. In this neighborhood, however, there came subsequently in a large number of Pennsylvania Germans, who have proved to be most excellent citizens, good farmers, industrious and economical. To them the county of Montgomery owes much of its high character and rapid growth. The following tabular statistics will give the reader a better idea of what Montgomery is, than a mere description:

Square Miles	480	
Number of acres	307,200	
Acres in Corn	36,454	
Corn produced	1,359,179	bushels.
Acres in Wheat	36,094	
Wheat produced	788,784	bushels.
Average Corn per acre	38	"
Average Wheat per acre	22	"
Tobacco shipped on the Miami Canal	792,152	lbs.
Number of Cattle	13,893	
" of Swine	31,921	
" of Horses	10,057	
" of Sheep	18,554	
Assessed value of Property	$13,498,514	
Assessed value to each family of 6 persons	2,140	

The assessed value of Moneys, Credits, and Personalties in this county is higher than any other one, except Hamilton. The above table shows that Montgomery is less productive than Butler, in Corn, and more productive in Wheat. The average per acre is less for Corn and more for Wheat. There are few districts in the United States, and few anywhere which produce as high an *average* per acre in wheat. The Corn land has been greatly diminished by the culture of Tobacco, fields of which we frequently see from the cars.

MIAMISBURGH—forty-nine miles from Cincinnati, and eleven from Dayton, is now in sight, on the other side of the river. This town has about 1,000 inhabitants. It is a flourishing country village, deriving its growth and importance from the rich farming country around. It has a Cotton Factory, two Founderies, several Mills, a variety of Stores, three Churches, and a High School.

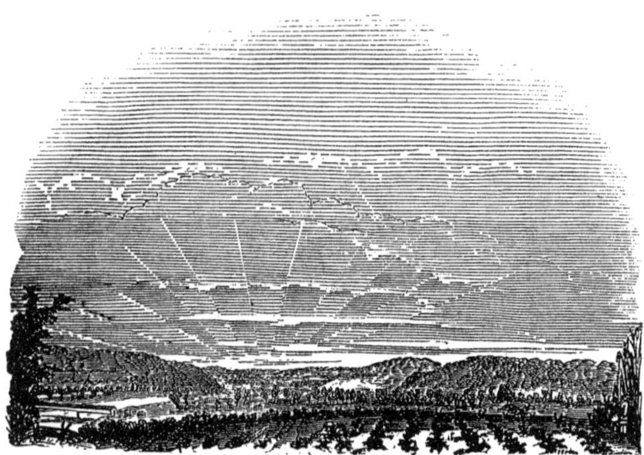

In the lower part of Miamisburgh, are the remains of an ancient work; and this region abounds in the works and fortifications so common in the West. About a mile and a quarter Southeast of the village, on an elevation more than 100 feet above the Miami, is the largest mound in the Northern States, excepting the mammoth mound at Grave-creek, on the Ohio, below Wheeling, which it about equals in dimensions. It measures about 800 feet around the base, and rises to the height of 67 feet. When first known, it was covered with forest trees, from the top of one of which—a maple tree growing from its apex—it is said, Dayton could be plainly seen. The mound has not been thoroughly examined, like that at Grave-creek; but probably is similar in character. Many years since, a shaft was sunk from the top; at first, some human bones were exhumed, and at the depth of about eleven feet, the ground sounding hollow, the workmen were afraid to progress farther. Probably two vaults are in it, like those of Grave-creek; one at the base in the center, the other over it, near the summit; it was, we suppose, this upper vault which gave forth the hollow sound. The mound is the steepest on the north and east sides, and is ascended with some little difficulty. It now sustains an orchard of about forty apple, and a few peach and forest trees. The view from the summit is beautiful. At one's feet lays the village of Miamisburgh, while the fertile valley of the river is seen stretching away for miles.

From this point to Dayton, the cars pass through a more picturesque scenery. The river may be seen, at times, just at our side, and surrounded by green foliage, having yet the original aspects of nature.

THE PINNACLES—just above Miamisburgh. If the traveller will look carefully to the left, he will see three *pinnacles*, like small pyramids, from thirteen to fifteen feet high. They look artificial, but are really made by gradual washing and attrition of particles, by the rain and atmosphere. They are composed of some hard clay, while the superincumbent earth has been loose and silicious. The consequence was, that, as the rains fell, the loose earth washed off; the sands fell away; the upper part of the clay wore away, till it fell into the shape of a natural pyramid. The wood cut gives a fair representation of their appearance.

THE RIVER SCENERY.—As we traverse this part of our road, we observe the Railway passes close by the side of the river. At one spot here, the stream has the appearance of a cl ar lake lying before us, embowered in circling hills and woods. The reader will recognize it in the accompanying cut.

THE TOBACCO SHEDS.—We have spoken of the large quantities of Tobacco raised in Montgomery county. The traveller will frequently observe long sheds, with Tobacco hanging in them.

These are the drying sheds, in which the plant, having been pulled, is hung up to dry. They are quite a novelty in this region, where tobacco has been cultivated only a few years.

Some of the most picturesque and beautiful scenery, to be viewed on any roads, is seen at various points along the Miami river, from Hamilton to Dayton, as the road recedes from, or approaches close to the banks; one of many of these views is seen in the cut below:

CARROLTON—fifty-two miles from Cincinnati, and eight miles from Dayton. This town is on the opposite side of the river, east from the Station. It is what is commonly called a "smart village," on the Miami Canal. It has a very large Distillery and Mills, from which great amounts of flour and whisky are shipped. The shipments from this place, Miamisburgh, and Middletown, are all entered at the Collector's office, Middletown. It may be interesting to notice the quantity of produce exported from that point. It will give some idea of the productiveness of this section of country.

Produce cleared at the Port of Middletown, 1851.

Flour	53,327 barrels.
Whisky	16,866 "

Corn	131,307
Wheat	7,366
Cheese	1,194,850 lbs.
Candles	39,538 "
Lard	571,611 "
Tobacco	345,524 "

These are dry facts, but they are certainly remarkable, for three country villages, which simply ship the produce of surrounding lands, without concentrating as ports of entry and cities do, the business of a large district. This is certainly a "land of bread," if of nothing else; nor is it wanting in "milk and honey"—for the rolling hills beyond, and the farm houses, out of sight, will give you the sweetest of milk and the sweetest of honey.

Dayton and Western Railroad.—We are now nearing Dayton. Just on our left hand we perceive the track of another Railroad, which soon curves to the west—very likely, we shall see the cars rolling off in the distance. This is the "Dayton and Western Railroad," which goes from Dayton to Greenville, Darke county. The distance is but thirty-six miles, and there is but one curve in it, and no grade over thirty feet. From Greenville to Dayton may be run in one hour. This road is now in course of extension to Union, a point on the Indiana State Line, (eleven miles from Greenville) where it will connect with the Indiana and Bellefontaine Railroad, running west to Indianapolis, and east to the Atlantic cities.

Miami Bridge.—We are now about to pass the Miami Bridge, over which both this and the Greenville Railways pass to reach the city of Dayton. By the way, speaking of bridges, there are five bridges over the Miami at Dayton, being on radiating roads from Dayton to various parts of the country. The river here makes nearly a semicircle, and by standing midway, all of them may be seen at once, while the town seems inclosed within the arch of the stream.

DAYTON—by card 59 80-100 miles from Cincinnati. By the time table, we have taken two hours and thirty minutes. Here, we must look around. This is a town which, in many respects, is one of the most beautiful and flourishing in the United States. It is the *fourth* town of Ohio, and the *fifty-ninth* of the Union, in magnitude, and is, therefore, in itself, an important place.

Seventeen days after the treaty of Greenville, on the 20th of August, 1795, ARTHUR ST. CLAIR, then Governor of the North-West Territory, JONATHAN DAYTON, formerly a Senator from New Jersey, JAMES WILKINSON, then an officer of WAYNE's army, and ISRAEL LUDLOW, of Long Hill, Morris county, New Jersey, whom we have already noticed, as the principal Pioneer of Cincinnati, purchased of JOHN CLEVES SYMMES, (the original patentee,) that part of the Miami in which Dayton lies. The first party who visited this site in 1795, were surveyors, of whom DANIEL C. COOPER, JOHN DUNLAP, and BENJAMIN VAN CLEVE, were a part.* On the 4th November, 1795, the town was laid out by ISRAEL LUDLOW, and called "Dayton," from one

* Curwen's History of Dayton.

of the proprietors. The first company of settlers consisted of nineteen persons only, who moved there from Cincinnati. Of these, GEORGE NEWCOM, still survives. He was an Irishman who came to America in 1775.

It seems the original settlers met no difficulties from the Indians. They had been well beaten by WAYNE, and were pacified by the treaty of Greenville. It was not till 1811, when, for the last time, they again rallied under the Prophet and TECUMSEH, to be forever vanquished, exiled, and destroyed from their native land. The Indians were quiet, but Judge SYMMES failed to make his payments, and the land reverted to the Government. By means of pre-emption rights and new agreements, DANIEL C. COOPER, one of the first settlers, became proprietor of Dayton.

Dayton was made the county seat of Montgomery county, (then first established,) in 1803, and at that time, there were only five or six families in the place, and but a very thin population anywhere in the Miami country. The first tavern was kept by GEORGE NEWCOM, who was also the first sheriff. The Court room was the second story of the tavern. Col. NEWCOM had a very novel mode of erecting jails and incarcerating prisoners. The Indians sometimes visited the whites and became troublesome. When in this condition, the High Sheriff of Montgomery county imprisoned them in his *corn crib!* In the case of whites, his method was entirely primitive and original. He had an old, unwalled well, and " there was no water in it." Into this he *let down* those who broke the peace of the State of Ohio, and there kept them, till they were *brought up* for trial!

This was Dayton, just half a century since—a half dozen straggling log-houses—a frame tavern, with a court-house in its upper room; another little village of log cabins at Franklin; and but here and there a family scattered through the beautiful country we have just passed through! Behold it now!

Dayton and the surrounding country has been immensely benefitted by the Miami Canal. The effect of it may be estimated by this fact, that prior to the completion of the Canal, the produce of this region was carried down the Miami river, in flat-boats, which took five or six days to reach Cincinnati, which the Railroad can reach in two hours and a half! These flat-boats could only navigate the river in the spring, and the navigation was often dangerous. The Canal was completed to

Dayton in January, 1829. This work at once gave a new impulse and extension to the business of Dayton. The country above rapidly improved; the produce shipped here greatly increased, manufactures began, and Dayton soon became a large town.

We are now in Dayton, and will glance at the town as it is. Before we do this, let us turn to a memorable event, which is in itself remarkable, and, in political annals, most extraordinary. This was the HARRISON meeting of 1840. The country was then full of political excitement, and the western country especially. It was the fashion of the day to call Mass Meetings—meetings in which the people gathered from every quarter, in great numbers. Whenever any popular orator was to address them, many thousands frequently assembled, and when General HARRISON was present, in Ohio and Indiana, immense masses of people were gathered. This was the case in 1840, at Dayton. It was in September, when the summer heats were abated, the woods began to be variegated, and a soft and hazy atmosphere was cast over nature, that General HARRISON was expected to enter Dayton, from the Springfield road. Every county was to be there, and every town in every county was to be represented. The day previous was occupied in the march from various towns to their rendezvous, and from that to Dayton. Every county had its band of music, and interspersed in the long trains of wagons, horses, and footmen, were log-cabins and canoes, the emblems of the Whig party. The sun rose bright on the expected day, and from the eminences around Dayton, with its white houses, its broad streets, its six hundred and forty-four flags, which waved from almost every house-top, the winding Miami, and the distant woods, all animated by tens of thousands of people, and all seen in one picturesque panorama, made one of the most beautiful and interesting scenes we ever beheld. At an early hour, before the procession could pass, hundreds and thousands, in wagons, horseback, and on foot, crowded on in advance, and the whole road became jammed with the masses. The procession from Springfield was supposed to number six thousand, and was headed by HARRISON and METCALFE (of Kentucky) finely mounted, and as it moved on, shouts rent the air, handkerchiefs waved from lovely hands, and music poured forth its notes. The meeting was held on the hill, east of where the Hydraulic Company's basin now is. The numbers were carefully computed by two gentlemen who measured the ground occupied by the crowd when addressed by HARRISON, and estimated the loose parties to be, in the aggregate, *one hundred thousand.* In 1842, the Convention which met Mr. CLAY is supposed to have been even more numerous.

The following are the principal features of Dayton at the present time.

THE HYDRAULIC WORKS. These are two-fold, the Cooper Hydraulics and the Dayton Hydraulic Company. The latter was established in 1845, by Messrs. PHILLIPS, BECKEL and EDGAR. They tapped the Mad river four miles above the town, and brought down its water over a fall of sixteen feet. These two hydraulic works furnish the city of Dayton with a great water-power, and have been of great service to its business and prosperity. The following manufacturing establishments are carried on by the Hydraulic works, viz:

6 Oil Mills,	3 Paper Mills,
7 Flour Mills,	4 Cotton Mills,
3 Woollen Factories,	6 Saw Mills,
1 Carpet Factory,	1 Car Factory,
5 Breweries,	1 Burr Millstone Factory.
8 Machine Shops,	1 Gun Barrel "

And several small establishments. Indeed, Dayton is really a manufacturing town. It concentrates for shipment a great quantity of produce; but it returns manufactured articles.

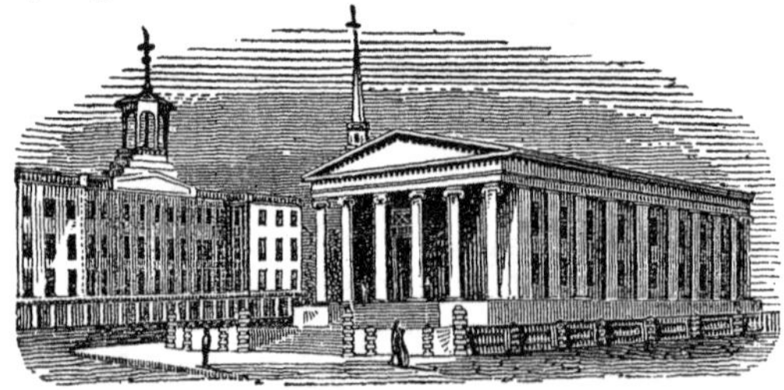

MONTGOMERY COURT HOUSE. This is the finest court house in the State, and would be deemed a fine architectural building in any State. It was built of Dayton marble, or rather of a fine limestone, found abundantly in this neighborhood. The building is fire-proof, with a marble roof, and the only wood used was for door and window frames. It is 127 feet long, by 62 in width. The court room is 42 by 50 feet, lighted by a dome, 43 feet from the floor. The style of architecture is shown in the preceding drawing.

One of the most imposing buildings which presents itself to the view of the stranger in the cars, is the County Jail, shown in the next engraving. This building has cost the county much money, and in connexion with the Court House, shows what a commendable public spirit exists in Dayton. From the "deep well," where prisoners were first incarcerated, or the miserably contrived prison which this has supplanted, we witness here an evidence of an advance in philanthropic feelings.

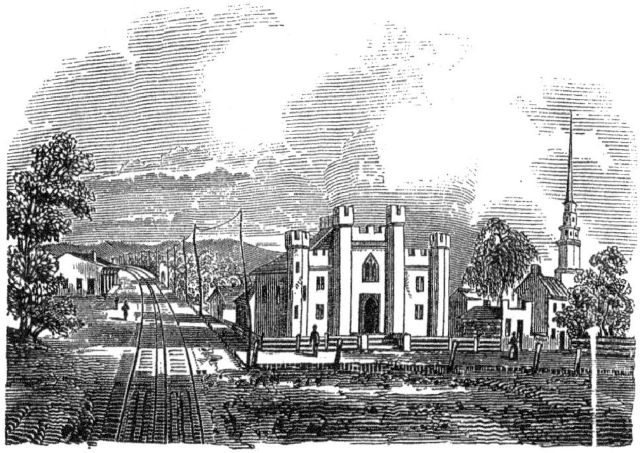

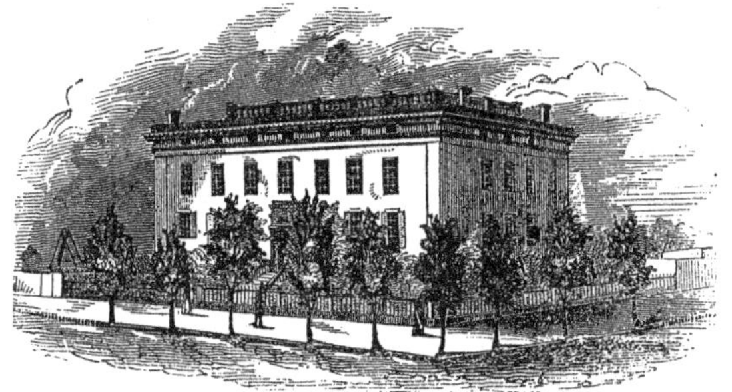

COOPER FEMALE ACADEMY.

The Cooper Female Academy is an institution much praised by the people of Dayton. The building is a handsome and commanding one, 84 feet by 54, three stories high. It has 175 pupils, under the management of Miss Margaret Coxe and Mr. Zachos, accomplished and well-known instructors.

The Phillips House is an extensive hotel, just erected, near the court house. It is an ornament, and will be very useful to the city. It was built by a company, and named after one of the principal citizens of Dayton. The building is seen in the drawing of the Court House.

Woodland Cemetery is on a hill on the south side of the town. It is one mile from the center of the town, contains forty acres of ground, and three miles of McAdamized road. It is finely improved, and commands one of the most beautiful views in the West. Dayton, its rich vale, winding river, and green fields lie below. The smoke of distant cars indicates the railways, while all around is silent, quiet, calm as the rest which attends the dead. Here sleep they, who never heard of cars and steamers, and all the whirl of the great world now rushing by. The cars thunder by, but they hear it not. In this beautiful mount they "sleep the sleep which knows no waking," till they are called by louder thunder, and raised to other worlds. The drawing gives a good view of one part of the Cemetery. On the line of the Railroad track, as seen in this view, is presented an imposing structure, in modern Gothic style, which is the county jail. We also present a view of the Railroad over the river, one of the best structures on the line.

The following statistics give a brief outline of what Dayton now is:

Population in 1850	10,956
Churches	23
District Schools	6
Market Houses	2
TURNPIKES	17

Dayton may be almost called the Turnpike City. It has *seventeen* turnpikes McAdamized, radiating in every direction from the town, and affording the utmost facilities of intercourse between the town and the agricultural population. Greenville, Covington, and Germantown on the west, Springfield, Xenia, Wilmington, Lebanon, on the east, with several other places, are connected with Dayton by fine McAdamized roads.

RAILROADS.—If Dayton is the Turnpike City, it promises soon to be a Railroad city. Six Railways are either already made or in course of construction, which will terminate or intersect here. They are as follows:

1. CINCINNATI, HAMILTON, and DAYTON, which we have just traversed.

2. MAD RIVER RAILROAD, which goes from Dayton to Springffeld, 25 miles, and thence to Sandusky city, 157 miles.

3. The GREENVILLE and MIAMI, which we have before mentioned—37 miles from Dayton to Greenville; thence to Union, ten miles; thence on the Indianapolis and Bellefontaine Railroad to Indianapolis.

4. The DAYTON and WESTERN, which passes out of Dayton, on a track with the Greenville road to junction; thence to the Indiana line, connecting with the Indiana Central Railroad, through Richmond and Centreville to Indianapolis.

5. The DAYTON and XENIA, 15 miles, to connect with the Little Miami Railroad, at Xenia. This is about to be commenced.

6. The DAYTON, TROY, and MICHIGAN RAILROAD. This goes north to Troy, Piqua, and is intended finally to reach the Michigan railways. From Dayton to Troy, 21 miles, is now being constructed.

MAD RIVER is the principal branch of the Great Miami, if, indeed it be not the main stream. It is called "Mad" from its rapid and mad-like current, which is more swift than any other stream in the State. It rises in Logan county, and after traversing Champaign and Montgomery, joins the Miami, just above. The lands, watered by Mad river and its tributaries, are among the best in Ohio. From Dayton to Springfield, 24 miles (which we are about to pass over) the Railway passes through its valley, and from the cars we may here glance at the Mad river country. The two counties of Clarke and Montgomery have an average of sixty-two inhabitants per square mile, which, for a State not fifty years old, does very well.

Osborne Station, ten miles from Dayton and fourteen miles from Springfield, we reach in about twenty minutes after leaving Dayton. The accompanying view is of the Station House and Railway:

Fairfield, twelve miles from Dayton and thirteen from Springfield, is a country village in one corner of Greene county, through which we have passed for four or five miles. It lies to the left of the Railway, and contains four churches and 400 inhabitants.

Clarke County Line, thirteen miles from Dayton. Here we enter upon the fine and flourishing county of Clarke, like those we have passed through, one of the best in the State. It is watered by Mad river, Buck creek and Beaver creek. Taken as a whole, it belongs to the great Table Land spreading from the Alleghanies to the Mississippi; but, as the traveller casts his eye around, he will see that it is gently undulating, and has that pleasant and convenient rolling, swelling surface which carries off the waters to its rapid streams, and leaves the land rich and beautiful. The following are its statistics, viz:

Square miles	412
Number of acres	262,680
Acres in Corn	24,591
Production of Corn	799,489 bushels.
Average per acre	32½ "
Acres of Wheat	23,488
Production of Wheat	491,954
Average per acre	20 bushels.
Cattle	11,943
Horses	6,553
Sheep	47,455
Swine	17,967
Population	22,136
Persons to a square mile	54
Assessed value of county	$7,099,288
Average value assessed to each family of six persons	$1,900

The number of Sheep in this county is much greater than in Butler and Montgomery, before mentioned, but, in other respects, it is neither so rich nor so productive.

ENON, seventeen miles from Dayton and eight from Springfield, is a country village, with two churches and three or four

hundred inhabitants. In the outskirts of the town may be seen a beautiful rising ground. The view in the sketch is of Ross's Mill, near Enon.

Hotkin's Mills, nineteen miles from Dayton and five from Springfield, are sketched in the wood cut.

Old Piqua, the birth place of Tecumseh, the last great warrior of the Aboriginals, is on the north (here the left) side of Mad river. We cannot hurry by this (not classical but *historical*) ground without saying something of the Great Chief.

Piqua was a name given by the Indians to several of their towns. It is the name of a Shawanee tribe, and signifies, "*a man formed out of the ashes.*" The origin of his name is one of those singular traditions, by which many of the most savage and ignorant nations preserve a dim and shadowy memory of some features of the primitive creation. The tradition is, that long time ago, the Shawanese nation was assembled at its Annual Feast and Thanksgiving. They were all seated round a large fire, which having burnt down, a great puffing was observed in the ashes, when, behold! a full-formed man came up out of the coals and ashes; and this was the first man of the Piqua Tribe!

We have already mentioned the expedition of General Clarke, destroying the Indian towns in 1780. Of the towns destroyed Piqua was the principal.

The old Indian town of Piqua, the ancient Piqua of the Shawanese, and the birth-place of Tecumseh, was situated on the north side of Mad river, about five miles west of Springfield, and occupied the site on which a small town called West Boston, has since been built. Drake's Life of TECUMSEH says:

"The principal part of Piqua stood upon a plain, rising fifteen or twenty feet above the river. On the south, between the village and the river, there was an extensive prairie—on the northeast, some bold cliffs terminating near the river—on the west and northwest, level timbered land; while on the opposite side of the stream, another prairie, of varying width, stretched back to the high grounds. The river sweeping by in a graceful bend—garnished with tall grass and brilliant flowers—combined to render the situation of Piqua both beautiful and picturesque. At the period of its destruction, Piqua was quite populous. There was a rude log hut within its limits, surrounded by pickets. It was, however sacked and burnt on the 8th of August, by an army of one thousand men, from Kentucky, after a severe and well-conducted battle with the Indians who inhabited it. All the improvements of the Indians, including more than two hundred acres of corn and other vegetables then growing in the fields, were laid waste and destroyed; and in defence of which they fought with the skill and valor characteristic of their nation."

OLD PIQUA.

The account appended of the destruction of Piqua by General GEORGE ROGERS CLARKE, was published twenty years since in BRADFORD'S Notes on Kentucky.

"On the 2d of August, 1780, General CLARKE took up the line of March from where Cincinnati now stands, for the Indian towns. The line of march was as follows:—the first division, commanded by CLARKE, took the front position; the center was occupied by artillery, military stores, and baggage; the second, commanded by Col. LOGAN, was placed in the rear. The men were ordered to march in four lines, at about forty yards distant from each other, and a line of flankers on each side, about the same distance from the right and left line. There was also a front and a rear guard, who only kept in sight of the main army. In order to prevent confusion, in case of an attack of the enemy, on the march of the army, a general order was issued, that in the event of an attack in front, the front was to stand fast, and the two right lines to wheel to the right, and the two left hand lines to the left, and form a complete line, while the artillery was to advance forwards to the center of the right line. In case of an attack on either of the flanks or side lines, these lines were to stand fast, and likewise the artillery, while the opposite lines wheeled and formed on the two extremes of those lines. In the event of an attack being made on the rear, similar order was to be observed as an attack in front.

"In this manner the army moved on without encountering anything worthy of notice until they arrived at Chillicothe, (situated on the Little Miami river, in Greene county,) about two o'clock in the afternoon, on the 6th day of August. They found the town not only abandoned, but most of the houses burnt down and burning, having been set on fire that morning. The army encamped on the ground that night, and on the following day cut down several hundred acres of corn; and about four o'clock in the evening took up their line of march for the Piqua towns, which were about twelve miles from Chillicothe, (in Clarke county.) They had not marched more than a mile from Chillicothe, before there came on a very heavy rain, with thunder and lightning and considerable wind. Without tents or any other shelter from the rain, which fell in torrents, the men were as wet as if they had been plunged into the river, nor had they it in their power to keep their guns dry. It was nearly dark before the rain ceased, when they were ordered to encamp in a hollow square, with the baggage and horses in the center—and, as soon as fires could be made, to dry their clothes, &c. They were ordered to examine their guns, and be sure they were in good order; and to discharge them in the following manner. One company was to fire, and time given to re-load, when a company at the most remote part of the camp from that which had fired, was to discharge theirs, and so on alternately, until all the guns were fired. On the morning of the 8th, the army marched by sunrise, and having a level, open way, arrived in sight of Piqua, situated on the west side of Mad river, about two o'clock, P. M. The Indian road from Chillicothe to Piqua, which the army followed, crossed the Mad river about a quarter of a mile below the town, and as soon as the advanced guard crossed into a prairie of high weeds, they were attacked by the Indians, who had concealed themselves in the weeds. The ground on which this attack, as well as the manner in which it was done, left no doubt but that a general engagement was intended. Col. LOGAN was therefore ordered, with about four hundred men, to file off to the right and march up the river on the east side, and to continue to the upper end of the town, so as to prevent the Indians from escaping in that direction, while the remainder of the men under Cols. LYNN, FLOYD, and HARROD, were ordered to cross the river and encompass the town on the west side, while Gen. CLARKE, with the troops under Col. SLAUGHTER, and such as were attached to the artillery, marched directly towards the town. The prairie in which the Indians were concealed, who commenced the attack, was only about two hundred yards across to the timbered land, and the division of the army, destined to encompass the town on the west side, found it necessary to cross the prairie to avoid the fire of a concealed enemy. The Indians evinced great military skill and judgment, and to prevent the western division from executing the duties assigned them, they made a powerful effort to turn their left wing. This was discovered by FLOYD and LINN, and to prevent being outflanked, they extended the line of battle west, more than a mile from the town, and which continued warmly contested on both sides until about five o'clock, when the Indians disappeared, everywhere unperceived, except a few in the town. The field-piece which had been entirely useless before, was now brought to bear upon the houses, when a few shot dislodged the Indians which were in them.

"A nephew of Gen. CLARKE, who had been many years a prisoner among the Indians, and who attempted to come to the whites just before the close of the action, was supposed to be an Indian, and received a mortal wound; but he lived several hours after he arrived among them.

"The morning after the battle, a Frenchman, who had been taken by the Indians a short time before, on the Wabash, and who had stolen away from them during the action, was found in the loft of one of the Indian Cabins. He gave the information that the Indians did not expect that the Kentuckians would reach their town on that day, and if they did not, it was their intention to have attacked them in the night, in their camp, with the tomahawk and knife, and not to fire a gun. They had intended to have made an attack the night before, but were prevented by the rain, and also the vigilance evinced by the Kentuckians in firing off their guns, and re-loading them, the reasons for which they comprehended when they heard the firing. Another circumstance showed that the Indians were disappointed in the time of their arriving; they had not dined. When the men got into the town, they found a considerable quantity of provisions ready cooked, in large kettles and other vessels, almost untouched. The loss on each side was about equal—each having about twenty killed.

"The Piqua town was built in the manner of the French villages. It extended along the margin of the river for more than three miles; the houses, in many places, were more than twenty poles apart. Col. LOGAN, therefore, in order to surround the town on the east, as was his orders, marched fully three miles, while the Indians turned their whole force against those on the opposite side of the town; and Logan's party never saw an Indian during the whole action. The action was so severe a short time before the close, that SIMON GIRTY, a white man, who had joined the Indians, and who was made a chief among the Mingoes, drew off three hundred of his men, declaring to them it was folly in the extreme to continue the action against men who acted so much like madmen as Gen. CLARKE's men, for they rushed in the extreme of danger, with a seeming disregard of the consequences. This opinion of GIRTY, and the withdrawal of the three hundred Mingoes, so disconcerted the rest, that the whole body soon after dispersed.

"It is a maxim among the Indians never to encounter a fool or a madman, (in which terms they include a desperate man,) for, they say, with a man who has not sense enough to take a prudent care of his own life, the life of his antagonist is in much greater danger than with a prudent man.

"It was estimated that at the two Indian towns, Chillicothe and Piqua, more than five hundred acres of corn was destroyed, as well as every species of eatable vegetables. In consequence of this, the Indians were obliged, for the support of their women and children to employ their whole time in hunting, which gave quiet to Kentucky for a considerable time.

"The day after the battle, the 9th, was occupied in cutting down the growing corn, and destroying the cabins and fort, &c., and collecting horses. On the 10th of August, the army began their march homeward, and encamped in Chillicothe that night, and on the 11th, cut a field of corn which had been left for the benefit of the men and horses on their return. At the mouth of the Licking, the army dispersed, and each individual made his best way home.

"Thus ended a campaign in which most of the men had no other provisions for twenty-five days, than six quarts of Indian corn each, except the green corn and vegetables found at the Indian towns, and one gill of salt; and yet not a single complaint was heard to escape the lips of a solitary individual. All appeared to be impressed with the belief, that if this army should be defeated, that few would be able to escape, and that the Indians then would fall on the defenceless women and children in Kentucky, and destroy the whole. From this view of the subject, every man was determined to conquer or die."

Tecumseh was the last great Shawanee. The Shawanese were the inhabitants of the Miami country, when the white men came to settle it, and it is right we should take some notice of the last great "brave" of that nation.

We subjoin a sketch of the Life of Tecumseh, derived from Drake's memoir of this celebrated chief:

"Puckeshinwa, the father of Tecumseh, was a member of the Kiskopoke, and Methoataske, the mother, of the Turtle tribe of the Shawanee nation; they removed from Florida to

Ohio, about the middle of the last century. The father rose to the rank of a chief, and fell at the battle of Point Pleasant, in 1774. After his death, his wife returned to the south, where she died at an advanced age. TECUMSEH was born at Piqua, about the year 1768, and, like Napoleon, in his boyish pastimes, showed a passion for war; he was the acknowledged leader among his companions, by whom he was loved and respected, and over whom he exercised an unbounded influence; it is stated, that the first battle in which he was, occurred on the site of Dayton, between a party of Kentuckians, under Col. BENJAMIN LOGAN, and some Shawanese. When about seventeen years of age, he manifested signal prowess, in an attack on some boats on the Ohio, near Limestone, Ky. The boats were all captured, and all in them killed, except one person, who was burnt alive. TECUMSEH was a silent spectator, never having witnessed the burning of a prisoner; after it was over, he expressed his strong abhorrence of the act, and by his eloquence persuaded his party never to burn any more prisoners.

"From this time, his reputation as a brave, and his influence over other minds increased, and he rose rapidly in popularity among his tribe; he was in several actions with the whites prior to WAYNE's treaty, among which was the attack on Fort Recovery, and the battle of the Fallen Timbers. In the summer of 1795, TECUMSEH became a chief; from the spring of this year until that of 1796, he resided on Deer Creek, near the site of Urbana, and from whence he removed to the vicinity of Piqua, on the Great Miami. In 1798, he accepted the invitation of the Delawares, then residing in part on White river, Indiana, to remove to that neighborhood with his followers. He continued in that vicinity a number of years, and gradually extended his influence among the Indians.

In 1805, through the influence of LAULEWASIKAW, the brother of TECUMSEH, a large company of Shawanees established themselves at Greenville. Very soon after, LAULEWASIKAW ssumed the office of a *Prophet;* and forthwith commenced that career of cunning and pretended sorcery, which enabled him to sway the Indian mind in a wonderful degree.

"Throughout the year 1806, the brothers remained at Greenville, and were visited by many Indians from different tribes, not a few of whom became their followers. The Prophet dreamed many wonderful dreams, and claimed to have had many supernatural revelations made to him; the great eclipse of the sun which occurred in the summer of this year, a knowledge of which he had by some means attained, enabled him to carry conviction to the minds of many of his ignorant followers, that he was really the earthly agent of the Great Spirit. He boldly announced to the unbelievers, that on a certain day, he would give them proof of his supernatural powers, by bringing darkness over the sun; when the day and hour of the eclipse arrived, and the earth, even at mid-day, was shrouded in the gloom of twilight, the Prophet, standing in the midst of his party, significantly pointed to the heavens and cried out, "Did I not prophesy truly? Behold! darkness has shrouded the sun!" It may readily be supposed that this striking phenomenon, thus adroitly used, produced a strong impression on the Indians, and greatly increased their belief in the sacred character of their Prophet."

In the spring of 1808, Tecumseh and the Prophet removed to a tract of land, on the Tippecanoe, a tributary of the Wabash. From that time till 1811, the brothers were stirring up and concentrating the Indians, preparatory to the final drama. In August, 1810, Tecumseh held a Council with Governor Harrison, at Vincennes. The Council broke up with hostile feelings on both sides. In July, 1811, the Chief again visited Governor Harrison, accompanied by three hundred warriors, but nothing resulted from the visit. In October following, Harrison, having warned the Indians to obey the Treaty of Greenville, marched up the Wabash. On the 7th of November following, he was attacked, by the Indians, at Tippecanoe, and defeated them.

In the commencement of the war of 1812, Tecumseh joined the British—was in the battle of Brownstown, and commanded at Maguaga. In the last action, he was wounded, and was appointed Brigadier General in the British army.

Death of Tecumseh.—"Tecumseh entered the battle of the Thames with a strong conviction that he should not survive it. Further flight he deemed disgraceful, while the hope of victory in the impending action was feeble and distant. He, however, heroically resolved to achieve the latter or die in the effort. With this determination he took his stand among his followers, raised the war-cry and boldly met the enemy. From the commencement of the attack on the Indian line, his voice was distinctly heard by his followers, animating them to deeds worthy of the race to which they belonged. When that well known voice was heard no longer above the din of arms, the battle ceased. The British troops having already surrendered, and the gallant leader of the Indians having fallen, they gave up the contest and fled. A short distance from where TECUMSEH fell, the body of his friend and brother-in-law, WASEGOBOAH, was found. They had often fought side by side, and now, in front of their men, bravely battling the enemy, they, side by side, closed their mortal career.

"Thus fell the Indian warrior, TECUMSEH, in the 44th year of his age. He was of the Shawanee tribe, five feet ten inches high, and with more than the usual stoutness, possessed all the agility and perseverance of the Indian character. His courage was dignified, his eye penetrating, his countenance, which, even in death, betrayed the indications of a lofty spirit, rather of the sterner cast. Had he not possessed a certain austerity of manners, he could never have controlled the wayward passions of those who followed him to battle. He was of a silent habit, but when his eloquence became roused into action by the reiterated encroachments of the Americans, his strong intellect could supply him with a flow of oratory that enabled him, as he governed in the field, so to prescribe in the council. Those who consider that in all territorial questions, the ablest diplomatists of the United States are sent to negotiate with the Indians, will readily appreciate the loss sustained by the latter in the death of their champion. Such a man was the unlettered savage, TECUMSEH, and such a man have the Indians lost forever. He has left a son, who, when his father fell, was about seventeen years old, and fought by his side. The prince regent, in 1814, out of respect to the memory of the old, sent out as a present to the young TECUMSEH, a handsome sword. Unfortunately, however, for the Indian cause and country, faint are the prospects that TECUMSEH, the son, will ever equal in wisdom or prowess, TECUMSEH, the father."

THE WATER STATION, represented in the engraving, is three and a half miles west of Springfield, and affords a pleasant natural scene.

THE DEEP CUT is 2½ miles from Springfield, and is an example of very heavy cutting.

THE BRIDGE OVER MAD RIVER, is two miles from Springfield, and gives a very pretty view.

THE CROSSING OF THE NATIONAL ROAD, one mile south of Springfield, is another pleasant view.

SPRINGFIELD.—We have now arrived at Springfield, 24 miles from Dayton, and 84 miles from Cincinnati. The first settlement of Springfield was made by DAVID LOWRY, of Pennsylvania, who settled at or near Springfield in 1795. In those days, bears, deer, and other wild game were very plenty here. In that season, Mr. LOWRY and his companion killed seventeen bears, and Mr. L. stated, that in his life he had killed 1,000 deer!

JAMES DEMENT was the first proprietor of the town, which was laid out in 1799.

Springfield is, as the traveller will observe, a beautiful country town, situated on the banks of Buck creek, (a branch of Mad river,) and in the midst of a lovely, rolling country. The following statistics of the town will give the reader a view of what his eye has not already informed him.

Springfield has a population, by the census of 1850, of 5,108, and the township of 2,203 more, making in all, 7,311, quite a large place for a county seat, of the interior. There are twelve churches in Springfield, making one to each 600 inhabitants, viz: three Lutheran Churches, two Presbyterian, three Methodist, one Baptist, one Episcopal, one Catholic, and one Congregational.

There is also a flourishing and well established College, Wittenburg College, sustained chiefly by the Lutherans. There is a High School, a Female Seminary, a Reading Room, two Banks, two Founderies, and Oil, Paper, Planing, Saw, and Flour Mills, with an extensive variety of stores and shops.

The NATIONAL ROAD passes through Springfield. The MAD RIVER AND LAKE ERIE RAILROAD, from Dayton to Sandusky, also passes through. The LITTLE MIAMI RAILROAD from Cincinnati, also unites here with the Mad River.

The SPRINGFIELD AND PITTSBURGH RAILROAD is in course of construction from this place to Delaware.

The SPRINGFIELD AND LONDON RAILROAD is also constructing to London, (Madison county), by which a connection will be made with Columbus.

Thus there will be five different routes, by which a person may leave Springfield for any part of the United States. In the midst of a fertile country, and with all these facilities of locomotion, Springfield will continue to be, as it is, a growing and inviting town. We must now bid farewell, for a time, to our companions, in the cars. We have accompanied you through as rich a country, by nature, as the world knows of, and we leave you in as charming a town as that country has! Farewell, for a time!

JUDGE BURNET.

Jacob Burnet (whose residence in Cincinnati is engraved on the last page of this work) was the son of Dr. Wm. Burnet, of New Jersey, and born February 22d, 1770. He was graduated at Nassau Hall, Princeton—admitted to the Bar of the Supreme Court of New Jersey, in 1796, and immediately proceeded to Cincinnati, where he has since resided. For nearly all his active life, he was a practising lawyer, but has served for several years as Judge of the Supreme Court, and as United States Senator in Congress. In social, political, and public life, he has always been distinguished—a man of perfect integrity and of eminent talents.

We copy here, two or three paragraphs from "Burnet's Letters," written by him for the Historical Society, as an illustration of what were the primitive customs—the antiquities of the Northwestern States.

"At that time the Northwestern Territory, so named by Congress, included the three northern States on the Ohio river, together with Michigan and the Ouisconsin Territory. The Governor had established four counties, each of which was sufficiently large to form an independent State. He had given them the names of Washington, Hamilton, St. Clair, and Knox, in honor of the distinguished patriots of the Revolution, whose names they bore, and who probably stood on the scale of merit, in the order in which they are named. The seats of justice for these counties were established at Marietta, Cincinnati, Kaskaskias, and Vincennes. Early in 1796, the British government surrendered the Northern posts, in pursuance of the treaty of 1793, to General WAYNE, who had been appointed for that purpose. Immediately after that important event, the governor established the county of Wayne, selecting that name as a compliment to the brave chief, whose victory, in 1794, at the rapids of the Miami of the Lake, had unquestionably hastened the surrender."

Detroit was the county seat of Wayne.

"If you look at the map of the Territory, and ascertain the situation of the seats of justice, in the several counties, as they existed at that time, and consider that the country was then an unbroken wilderness, without roads, and destitute of a white population, except in the immediate vicinity of the county towns, you will be ready to conjecture, that the legal business of each county, was transacted by such professional men as resided in it. Such, however, was not the fact. From the year 1796, till the formation of the State government, in 1803, I attended the general Court at Cincinnati, Marietta, and Detroit, regularly, and never missed a term during that period. The jaunts between those remote places, through a wilderness country, in its primitive state, were attended with exposure, fatigue and hazard. We generally travelled in parties of two or three, or more, and took a pack-horse to transport such necessaries as our own horses could not conveniently carry; for no dependence could be placed for supplies on the route. Though we frequently passed through Indian villages, they were too poor to afford assistance. Sometimes we could purchase from them small quantities of corn for the use of our horses, but even this relief was not to be depended on.

In performing these journeys, either in summer or winter, the traveller was compelled to swim every water-course in his route, which could not be forded. The country being destitute of bridges and ferries, as well as roads, we had to rely on our horses as the only substitute; and it sometimes happened, that after swimming a stream covered with floating ice, we had to encamp on the ground for the night. This consideration made it common for a person, when purchasing a horse, to ask the question, whether he was a good swimmer; which was considered one of the most valuable qualities of a saddle-horse. I recollect, in the fall of 1801, on my return, without company, from the general court at Marietta, it rained almost incessantly, during the whole journey, which subjected me to the necessity of swimming four or five times on my horse, once at White-Oak, with evident peril of life. That stream was higher than I have ever seen it before or since. The bottom on the east side was entirely covered with water. When I came to the edge of it, I paused for some time, to ascertain whether the water was rising or falling; on being satisfied of the former, I determined to proceed. For the purpose of keeping my papers dry, they were taken from my saddle-bags, and tied behind me on the top of my cloak. The opposite bank was a bluff, having a narrow way cut down to the creek, where the path crossed it, for the use of travellers. After estimating the velocity of the current as well as I could, by motion of the drift-wood, for the purpose of deciding how far I should enter above the landing place, in order to strike it, I put in with the head of my horse a little up-stream, he however chose to steer for himself, and made directly for the landing. Being a fine swimmer, he struck it at the lower point, so as to enable me to grasp a bush, by which I was able to assist him in extricating us both from the threatening danger. I rose the bank with a light heart, and proceeded on my way to Williamsburgh, where I swam the East-fork, rather than wait for a canoe from the opposite side. The next morning, I swam it again near where Batavia now stands, and the same day arrived safely at home."

Of the Pioneers of Cincinnati, Judge BURNET is the oldest Statesman; Dr. DANIEL DRAKE, the oldest Physician; JAMES FERGUSON, the oldest Merchant; and NICHOLAS LONGWORTH, (founder of the vineyards,) after Judge BURNET, the oldest Lawyer.

THE CINCINNATI GAZETTE,

Daily, $8.00, Tri-Weekly, $5.00, Weekly, $2 per annum.

THE HISTORY OF THE GAZETTE, AND THE CHANGES IN THE PAPER, THE PLACE, AND PEOPLE.

On the 25th of June, 1825, was commenced a new volume of the DAILY GAZETTE and of the LIBERTY HALL AND CINCINNATI WEEKLY GAZETTE. We deem it a fitting time to make some remarks as to the history of the paper, and the history of the North-West Territory, which has passed from a wilderness to a country of *States*, teeming with millions of population, and evidencing a prosperous and enlightened community.

On the 9th of November, 1793, the first newspaper was established in the North-West Territory, by Wm. Maxwell, and called the *Centinel of the North West Territory*, as it was indeed a wilderness, without the range of civilization, and within the land of savages. At the time of the establishment of this paper, Cincinnati was in the range of the Indians, and some are yet amongst us who, when their huts were building, watched the woods, rifle in hand, to keep the workmen from being scalped. Mr. Ferguson informs us, that whilst the choppers were cutting down the trees in the North-East part of the city to build his cabin, corner of Third and Main, he stood as sentinel, or ranged the forest rifle in hand. One of the Indians informed a citizen in after days, that he used to watch the movements of the early settlers from the limbs of the trees on Mount Adams.

The Cincinnati Gazette is a regular descendant by transfer of subscription list from this first paper, although the name and immediate papers are of subsequent date; the Gazette derives its name by original date to this day. In 1796, the original paper changed its name to Freeman's Journal, in consequence of the sale to E. Freeman. On the 28th May, 1799, the Western Spy and Hamilton Gazette was established, and on the 9th December, 1804, the publication of the Liberty Hall was commenced, a title still retained in our Weekly, and by which it is yet only known to many of our country readers. On the 15th July, 1815, T. Palmer commenced publishing the Gazette; but on the 11th December, 1815, he sold out and united with the Liberty Hall, and thereafter the paper was known as the Liberty Hall and Cincinnati Gazette. On the 25th June, 1827, this city, as yet had no Daily, though claiming a population of 19,000 people. It was suggested to the proprietors that a daily should be issued, and Messrs. E. Morgan and his co-partner canvassed the city to ascertain whether they could get patrons enough to sustain the enterprise, and having obtained in this population of 19,000 the number of 164 subscribers to a daily, they commenced publishing a Daily, under the abreviation of Daily Cincinnati Gazette, and it has continued till this day.

The Gazette has now subscribers who have been regular readers since the beginning. The changes which have been wrought in the country have been beyond those often witnessed by living men—the changes which have been wrought in the Gazette, its appearance, its news, its expenses, and its business, have been equally great. In the files of the Gazette will be found a history of the wilderness—the incoming of millions of people, and the most important events in our local history. Amongst the events, the beginning of which are noted, we may briefly state

The first paper issued.
First book published.
July 5, 1814, first Steamboat arrival announced,
March 3, 1816, first laying out of Covington.
1815, first steamboat built at Cincinnati launched.
Feb. 1, 1816, first Iron Foundery.
Aug. 1, 1816, first agitation of Gas works, by Wm. Greene.
Oct., 1818, first Circulating Library,
1819, first passenger steamer, Gen. Pike, built—100 feet keel, 14 state rooms, and provision for eighty-six passengers.
1839, first Free Soil paper issued.

The changes in proprietors and leading editors of the Gazette, considering the length of time it has been published, have been comparatively few. Prior to 1822, and for some years, Isaac G. Burnet, Esq. was editor, when he gave way to B. F. Powers, (brother of the sculptor,) who continued until 1825, when he was succeeded by, Charles Hammond, who occupied the place, being almost sole editor, till his death, April 3, 1840, he was succeeded, at his request, made known before his death, by John C. Wright, the present senior editor.

With the change of times has come a change in the publisher's business, equally material—a change in the mode of getting news, a change in the amount of reading to satisfy an enlightened and commercial community, and a change in expense. Changes generally against the publisher, as the cost of a weekly paper, the cost of a daily paper, and the cost of an advertisement have continued the same; although many hundred per cent. of expense has been added. The original subscribers have always paid us their $2 for the Weekly, or their $8 for the Daily. Some of these changes it may be interesting to note.

We cannot go back into description further than 1804, when we find the *Liberty Hall*, issued from the cock-loft of a log-cabin, situated on the slope of the hill, about twenty feet above the present grade of the street, on the south-east corner of Sycamore and Third streets. The paper was royal size, and the entire work—editing, composition, press-work, distributing, mailing, and collecting, was chiefly done by Rev. Mr. Browne, the proprietor, with time to preach and do other jobs. The price of the paper was $2, the entire expense about $15. At this time, we find the latest news received, was from London, in three months, and from New York in one month. The favorite route East to the "Old Settlements," as the Atlantic was called by Mr. Ferguson, (still living,) was on horse-back, via Cumberland Gap and the Virginia Valley. The changes in style and expense have been continuous and constant.

On the 25th June, 1827, when the first Daily was begun, the facilities for news were not very great—New York was a great way off, and mails the only resource—slow and uncertain. The expenses of publication about $40 per week, and the size superroyal. In 1835, in order to show the change wrought, an entire paper of January 11, 1794, was transferred into the Gazette, and made then but four and one-fourth columns, or one-seventh of the then Daily. If a transfer were now made, the first Daily would not make much, if any, over one-seventh of the present Daily.

The change in the labor of getting up a paper has been equally great. At first, and even till about 1840, but one editor was necessary, and but few compositors. A job-office, necessary to keep, to attend to customers, as a distinct office would not pay for itself. The Gazette, not content with mails, was the first, as a regular part of their business—to run an express to obtain early news. It was continued till the telegraph annulled all such enterprises. The city changed so rapidly from a village to a great commercial mart, as to require a special City or Local Editor, and in 1842, John B. Russell was first detailed on this duty. Since then we have had to have a Commercial Editor, and this branch of expense embraces about one-fifth of all. We have now about 200 exchange papers, and require four Editors for foreign news and two City Editors.

For near one-fourth of a century a single hand press and a single pressman were all that were needed. In 1834, the first power press ever brought west of the mountains, we believe, was brought out by the Gazette, and in 1841 the first Hoe Cylinder Press for a daily paper. In early times the Gazette forms were locked and the paper off the press by early bed time—now there is no hour of the day or night that persons are not at work getting out the paper. At one o'clock, A. M., seven hands find employment at the *presses* whilst *one* used to answer.

Instead of using the cock-loft of a log cabin, with hand press and case to do the editing, composing, press work and distributing, we now have a six story building fully occupied—seven power presses at work—printing, press work, binding, engraving, &c., &c. done, 100 persons employed, and our expenses increased from $30 a week to over $150 per day.

Such are the changes in this feature of the business, and we may say to the patrons of the Gazette, that the quantity of matter for the same price has duplicated, and the ems of composition, the only test of the amount of reading—has changed since 1849 from 24,000 to 95,000. The Gazette furnishes materially more than any other of its cotemporaries. We find on examination that the city daily papers measure as follows:

Sun contains	85,0[illegible]0 ems.
Atlas	161,000 "
Nonpareil	187,000 "
Commercial	199,000 "
Times	220,000 "
Enquirer	224,000 "
Gazette	382,000 "

We are gratified to state that our business, our circulation and advertisements have never been greater or better than now. We have patrons who have stood by the office unwaveringly for half a century, and we may say, generally, that we rarely lose a subscriber, and that counting from months to months, as far back as our books are at hand to examine, we find we always have enlarged our list of subscribers, and our circle of advertisers; and the gain in our subscription list daily and weekly, and of advertisers, has been greater the past six months than ever before.

For the success which has attended our efforts—for the confidence and patronage of our friends, we are thankful. To those who are interested in the progress of this Establishment—to the fast friends, new and old, who feel an interest in us, we have believed that this statement was due, and that it might be interesting to others. We shall continue to move onward—always improving; always meeting the wishes in view of an enlightened community as far as possible; always advocating sound principles, and the interest of the city and the West; always promoting the Whig cause, as the cause of the country; but not as the follower of any man or men—not influenced by temporary excitements—not changing for local influences. We shall endeavor, as always, to pay respect to the opinions of others, and differing, to do so as may be due from gentlemen to gentlemen. Courteous to all—following the behests and dictations of none.

CINCINNATI, July 22, 1852.

PART II.

Descriptive and Illustrative, of the Little Miami, the Xenia and Columbus, and the Columbus and Cleveland Railways, will be published in a few weeks.

NOTE.—This is one of the sections of the several Railroads of Ohio, which will be embraced in the Guide Book. It is purposed as fast as the work can be got through the press, to embrace all the Railroads of the State of Ohio. The sketches of the greater number of the roads, are complete, and the others are progressing as fast as possible. The engraving and stereotyping, consume much more time than was anticipated. The next section, Cincinnati to Springfield and Cleveland, will be complete in a few weeks, and the others, in their successive connection, will follow. We are arranging also, for the Railroads of Indiana, on account of the connection of these roads with those of Ohio.

Should this book fall into the hands of any, who see errors in the facts stated, we will be obliged for any correction. We shall, also, be grateful for any local incidents, in the history of the country along the line of any of the Railroads in Ohio and Indiana, built or building.

THE OHIO RAILROAD GUIDE:

ILLUSTRATED AND DESCRIPTIVE,

CONTAINING

TOPOGRAPHICAL, BIOGRAPHICAL, AND STATISTICAL NOTICES OF THE COUNTIES, TOWNS, AND SCENERY,—WITH BRIEF SKETCHES OF PUBLIC MEN:

BEING A

TRAVELLING COMPANION THROUGH OHIO.

CINCINNATI:
CINCINNATI GAZETTE COMPANY PRINT.
1852.

THE

OHIO RAILROAD GUIDE:

ILLUSTRATED AND DESCRIPTIVE.

PART II.

LITTLE MIAMI,—COLUMBUS & XENIA,—AND CLEVELAND & COLUMBUS RAILWAYS.

From Cincinnati to Cleveland.

CINCINNATI:
CINCINNATI GAZETTE COMPANY PRINT.
1852.

GUIDE BOOK.

DISTANCES.

BUFFALO, N. Y. TO NEW YORK.

Attica and Buffalo R. R.

Lancaster,	10	
Alden	10	20
Darien,	5	25
Attica	6	31

Tonnawonda R. R.

Alexander,	3	34
Batavia,	8	42
Byron,	7	49
Bergen,	7	56
Churchville,	4	60
Rochester,	14	74

Auburn and Rochester R. R.

Brighton,	4	78
Pittsford,	4	82
Victor,	12	94
Canandaigua,	9	103
Chapinsville,	3	106
Short's Mills,	3	109
Clifton Springs,	5	114
West Vienna,	3	117
East Vienna,	1	118
Oak's Corners,	3	121
Geneva,	5	126
Waterloo	7	133
Seneca Falls,	4	137
Cayuga Bridge,	5	142
Auburn,	10	152

Auburn and Syracuse R. R.

Sonnet,	5	157
Skaneateles Junction,.	4	161
Elbridge,	1	162
Camillus,	8	170
Geddes	6	176
Syracuse,	2	178

Syracuse and Utica R. R.

Manlius,	10	188
Chittenango	4	192
Conastota	6	198
Wampsville,	3	201
Oneida Depot,	3	204
Verona Centre,	4	208
Rome,	9	217
Oriskany,	7	224
Whitesboro',	4	228
Utica,	3	231

Utica and Schenectady R. R.

Schuyler,	8	239
Herkimer	7	246
Little Falls,	6	252
St. Johnsville,	10	262
Palatine Church,	3	265
Fort Plain,	3	268
Palatine Bridge,	3	271
Spraker's,	3	274
Fonda,	8	282
Tribes Hill,	6	288
Amsterdam	5	293
Cranesville,	4	297
Hoffman's,	3	300
Schenectady	9	309

Mohawk and Hudson R. R.

Albany	16	325

Steamboat on the Hudson.

New York,	145	470

Western R. R.

Boston,	200	525

CLEVELAND TO BUFFALO, N. Y.

By Steamboat.

Station	Miles	Total
Fairport,	30	
Ashtabula,	33	63
Conneaut	14	77
Erie, Pa.,	30	107
Dunkirk, N. Y.	48	155
Buffalo	43	198

CLEVELAND TO PITTSBURGH, PA.

Station	Miles	Total
Newburgh,	6	
Bedford,	6	12
Twinsburgh,	7	19
Hudson,	5	24
Franklin Mills,	10	34
Ravenna,	6	40
Edinburgh,	6	46
Palmyra,	5	51
Frederick	5	56
Ellsworth,	6	62
Canfield,	6	68
Boardman,	6	74
Poland	3	77
New Middletown,	5	82
Petersburgh	4	86
Enon Valley, Pa.	6	92
Darlington,	4	96
Beaver,	12	108
Freedom	3	111
Economy	7	118
Sewickly Bottom,	3	121
Alleghany,	14	135
Pittsburgh,	1	136

CLEVELAND TO TOLEDO.

Station	Miles	Total
Ohio City,	1	
Rockport	7	8
Dover,	5	13
North Ridgeville,	7	20
Elyria,	4	24
Amherst,	8	32
Henrietta	3	35
Birmingham,	3	38
Florence,	3	41
Berlinville,	4	45
Milan,	8	53
Norwalk,	4	57
Monroesville,	4	61
Four Corners,	3	64
Lyme,	3	67
Bellevue,	3	70
Green Creek,	10	80
Lower Sandusky,	8	88
Black Swamp,	8	96
Woodville,	7	103
Stony Ridge,	7	110
Perrysburgh,	9	119
Maumee City,	1	120
Toledo,	10	130

COLUMBUS TO PORTSMOUTH.

Station	Miles	Total
South Bloomfield,	17	
Circleville,	9	26
Chillicothe,	21	47
Waverley,	15	62
Piketon,	4	66
Lucasville,	14	80
Portsmouth,	12	92

GUIDE BOOK

OF

THE OHIO RAILWAYS.

CINCINNATI.

CINCINNATI is one of the Wonders of the West. Seventy years ago, on the site where now is the fifth city of the United States, exhibiting all the evidence of high civilization—there was a lonely forest, in the midst of which appeared a few solitary mounds—remains of an unknown people. Such a contrast is nowhere to be found; those cities of our country which are larger in size, or equally rapid in growth, are all of older date. None of so recent origin have such strength and magnitude. It is here, then, that we find one of the most striking examples of rapid development from the Savage to the Civilized state. The natural scenery around—hills, river and plain, are all associated, even in the memory of a single life, with the extremes of the wild forest, in the Past, and the thickly populated city of the Present.

At the close of the Revolution, the site of Cincinnati was on the war path of the Shawanees, and other Indian tribes, as they passed from their settlements on the Scioto and Miamis to the interior of Kentucky. The mouth of the Licking, opposite Cincinnati, was a land mark on their route. There, also assembled, in 1780, the army of General CLARKE, in the first successful expedition against the Indians of the Scioto, at Chil-li-co-the, and Pickaway. It was from a volunteer in that army—a celebrated pioneer—SIMON KENTON—that the county which contains the city of Covington, was recently named. Where Cincinnati is, there was not then even an Indian village. The only works of man seen amidst the solitary forests, were those mysterious mounds and solitary ramparts, which indicated a once populous country, but of whose people and character, not a remnant, nor a tradition remains. Lofty trees had grown and fallen upon them, when the Shawanee pursued his enemies on the war-path of the Licking; but no voice from those ancient tombs told by whom, or for what they were raised! The shadows of time flitted over them, and Mystery returned no answer to the question of Curiosity; the Indians seem to have simply regarded them as monuments, and beyond that to have had little interest in them.

After the settlement of Cincinnati, some curious young men opened one of the mounds, but found little except human bones, some pieces of copper, lead, and coal, and some very rude sculpture.* These monuments and works were situated in the very heart of the present city. One mound stood at the corner of Main and Third streets, the most valuable lot in the town; another was on Fifth street, below Western Row. Between Walnut and Race, Third and Fifth streets, was one of those circular ramparts, or fortifications, as they are usually called, so frequently found among the ancient remains of the West; another was between Broadway and Sycamore, near Fourth. These works seem to prove that Cincinnati was, in days beyond memory, what it now is: the populous residence of the then occupants of Ohio. But between that period and that of the white settlers, darkness rests upon all surrounding objects. We know that the forest has grown up on these works of an ancient people; and that the city has again replaced the forest, and on the ruins of the monuments, built the marts of commerce, and the abodes of civilization; but of the shadowy space between, we have neither history, tradition, nor memory.

It was nearly ten years after George Rogers Clarke and Simon Kenton had crossed the mouth of the Licking on their victorious march to the Shawanese towns of the Scioto, that a small band of sixteen persons left Maysville, (then called Limestone,) for the present Cincinnati. It was in the cold month of December, 1788. The sky was dark, the river was filled with running ice, and the shores lowered with inhospitable savages. Such scenes and dangers, however, were familiar to the bold pioneers, and after two or three days struggling in the ice, Ludlow and his companions landed safely opposite the Licking.

The spot, now Cincinnati, was within the patent of John

* Drake's "Picture of Cincinnati," 1815.

Cleves Symmes, who, in the year previous, had issued a pamphlet, proclaiming the future settlement of this country, and that such was the amazing fertility of the land, he actually believed, it was worth a silver dollar per acre! Attracted by such representations, Matthias Denman, of New Jersey, purchased an interest in "Symmes' Grant," and "located" the section and fractional section, (about eight hundred acres,) on which Cincinnati is now built. He then sold them to Patterson and Filson, and in August, 1788, they agreed to lay out a town. Soon after this, however, Filson, who had come out to Kentucky, was killed by the Indians, and his share transferred to Israel Ludlow, who thus became the first leader, and pioneer, among the settlers of Cincinnati.

It was a cold season, and Nature was clad in her wildest array, when his little band landed amidst forest trees, under the shadow of those olden mounds, but there was no shadow on their mind. They dreamed of the beautiful future; a town to be built on lands that were positively worth a silver dollar per acre,* must certainly make the fortunes of all who first adventured within its golden precincts. In their dreams there was something of the ludicrous, as well as the sublime. Before they set out from the sands of New Jersey, the town of their imagination must have a *name!* Filson, one of the original three in the project was a schoolmaster, and his genius was appealed to for the much wanted name. The appeal was not in vain; he gave a name, in August, 1788, before the settlers had left their homes, which was at once unique and *original.* He called the embryo town Losantiville! The name, on being analyzed, is supposed to be made up of four different languages, namely, "L," (Licking,) English—*os*, Greek—*anti*, Latin—and *ville*, French! It signifies "The town opposite the mouth of the Licking," and by this name is spoken of by Judge Symmes. It seems, however, never to have been given to the real town, for when Ludlow came to survey and record the village, it was called Cincinnati.† It commenced with half a dozen log cabins, and in 1796—seven years after—was still composed of log cabins, and perhaps a dozen rough frame houses, with stone chimneys. Not a brick had been seen in the place.

---

* Burnet's Letters. † Ibid.

In June, 1789, Major DOUGHTY, of the United States Army, arrived at Cincinnati and commenced the erection of a block house, called "FORT WASHINGTON," which gave the first impulse to the settlement, and was the rendezvous of the army and the United States officers during the next ten or fifteen years. The early settlers naturally collected around it for safety and society, during the war of the North West. The times were wild and dangerous, but in the "Fort," as in the old Feudal Castle, the brave and adventurous spirits dispelled all thoughts of gloom in the bowl, the song, or the dance. Many a gallant soldier and courteous gentleman, many a refined and elegant lady, gave as much of charm and zest to this camp in the wilderness, as if it had been a court in Europe. Here the high-minded ST. CLAIR, the heroic WAYNE, the young and impulsive HARRISON, and the fascinating WILKINSON, and others since conspicuous in history, formed a delightful circle enjoying the pleasures of intellectual and cheerful converse. Much of the history and spirit of that time may be found in the "Letters" of Judge BURNET, who, having mingled in those scenes and events, yet survives to see the Metropolis of the West sprung up, dream-like, where the mound, the forest, and the Fort once stood!

FORT WASHINGTON.

FORT WASHINGTON was on the brow of the slight hill, separating the upper from the lower plain of the town, and where Third street now runs from Broadway to Ludlow street. The front parapet was a little south of the south line of Third, and the flag-staff was placed at just about the intersection of Third and Ludlow. From 1790 to the Greenville treaty, in 1795, the settlers were obliged to keep close within, or near the defences of the fort; for the whole neighborhood was scoured with hostile Indians. They watched from the tops of the surrounding hills. Mount Adams, where the Observatory now is, just to the north-east of the site of Fort Washington, was then an Observatory for the Indians, as it now is to the Astronomers. On its top was a large and magnificent oak; in that tree, WHITE EYES, an Indian chief, subsequently told a lady in the fort, he had often watched, concealed by its foliage, the operations of the Garrison. He could see every motion, and knew every thing that was going on. Men were cut down in the very precincts of the garrison, and the woods resounded with the war whoop of the savage, and the wails of the dying. These dangers, however, did not last long. The treaty of Greenville, following the victory of WAYNE, terminated the conflict. Peace restored the hopes, and commenced the prosperity of Cincinnati. In 1805, an emigration from Baltimore gave a new impulse to the town, and in 1807, the Surveyor General of the United States surveyed into lots the sixteen acres which had been reserved by the Government around Fort Washington, and they were sold to individuals at public auction. Strangers who walk up the well built and spacious "Broadway"—a noble street—perceive that at Fourth street it is narrowed down to the common width, and frequently ask "Why was this; why not continue this broad avenue through the town?" The truth is, it is only due to the Government that there was any street of such breadth. The Fort Washington Reservation extended from the river, east of the public quay, to Fourth street, and its western boundary was Broadway, which the Surveyor General voluntarily made one hundred feet broad.

The sale of Fort Washington and its lands, in lots, may be said to terminate the primitive or pioneer period of Cincinnati. Time enough has passed since, (brief as it is in comparison with that of older cities,) to make the reminiscences of that period interesting, and causing its memorials to be gathered up and looked upon as antiquities! The races of the Mounds and Forts were ancient and extinct hundreds of years ago. The race of Red Men, old long since, are gone, scarcely remembered, and almost unknown to the present inhabitants. And now the Pioneers of yesterday are ancient; their grave yards are removed, their dwellings have disappeared, their traditions are sought out, and the stately mansions of ease and elegance rise where the log cabin and the rough frame once were:

> "Time rolls his ceaseless course. The race of yore,
> Who danced our infancy upon their knee,
> And told our marvelling boyhood legend's store
> Of their strange ventures, happed by land or sea,
> How are they blotted from the things that be!"

Of the Pioneer period of Cincinnati, enough has been preserved in various accounts, to give a very vivid and distinct picture of its appearance, manners, and growth. As we walk round the city, the natural turn of the grounds, the curved hills, the flowing river, and even the present streets, are all so associated with what was the Cincinnati of 1790–1800, and what it now is, that the story can be read as we go. It is true that the ancient mounds are obliterated; of Fort Washington there is no trace; that the alder swamps on the hill are forgotten, the shades of Deer Creek faded like fairy dreams, and the graves of Pioneers surmounted with the spires of lofty churches, and the splendid marts of merchandize. But yet the ground and the original plat of the town remain, and we can retrace the faded picture with the colors of memory.

Deer Creek, of which we spoke, is on the east side of the town, and winds round the base of Mount Adams, from whose summit the Observatory is visible from every quarter. The traveller who arrives by the Little Miami Railroad, seeks out the creek, and sees the outlet of the State's Miami Canal, having its other extreme at Toledo, on Lake Erie, but looks in vain for the creek. The creek is carried through an arched culvert, the earth is filled up over, and dwellings and workshops surmount. He crosses the mouth on a stone bridge, and usually hastens by an omnibus, along Second street, (Columbia,) to one of the principal hotels. In doing this, he crosses what is called the "Third Ward," included between Third street and the river on the lower plain. Nearly every foot of this space is now actively employed in business, but the stranger will be surprised to learn, it was originally, for the most part, a pond. The pond was frozen in winter, and on its ice, the few boys of the town found sport in skating, while in the spring, the wild duck floated on its bosom! Above (on Third street,) was Fort Washington, while the pond stretched from Broadway to Deer Creek below, and the principal part of the town was between Broadway and Main street. Deer Creek, a small rivulet, along whose banks the Miami Canal may now be seen, was enveloped, on the surrounding slopes, with a dense forest. In the spring floods, the boys would go up the little stream in canoes and gather flowers, or throw clubs at the turtles, sunning themselves on logs. Near Pike street, where are now the fine mansion and beautiful gardens of NICHOLAS LONGWORTH, Esq., "on the very spot where the people now go to watch the unfolding of the night blooming cereus, grew the red bud, crab apple, and gigantic tulip tree, or yellow poplar, with wild birds above, and native flowers below."* Proceeding, on the lower plain of the city, by Second or Front streets, we arrive in succession, at Broadway, Sycamore, and Main streets, in front of what is now the Public Landing. The landing, which is now so finely paved, and gently graded, and which is crowded with the materials of commerce, had then no existence. The *common* stretched out to the natural bank of the river, which was high, steep, and crumbling. Under it were moored the flat-boats or "arks" of the river traders, who came from Fort Pitt, Wheeling, and other towns, to dispose of their apples, flour, or whisky, below. On Front street, near the corner of Sycamore, was the "Tavern" of GRIFFIN YEATMAN, Esq., the first hotel keeper of Cincinnati! This worthy man lived to within two or three years since—was long Recorder of the county, and died respected—having nearly spanned, in his single life, the whole existence of Cincinnati!

This hotel often received distinguished guests, whose business or curiosity led them through the wilds of the West. In 1796, Judge BURNETT relates,† he met there the celebrated writer and traveller, VOLNEY, who had traversed Kentucky on foot, and carried his wardrobe in an oil cloth! He afterwards published

* DRAKE'S Discourse.

† BURNET'S Letters.

his observations, accompanied by philosophical reflections on the region of the Ohio.

Opposite the mouth of Sycamore street, near YEATMAN's hotel, "There was a small wooden market house built over a cove, into which pirogues and other craft, when the river was high, were poled or paddled, to be tied to the rude columns."* In Main street, below the hill, were a few shops, and it was not uncommon to see the wolf or panther brought in by the hunters; or, occasionally, as wild men of the woods, looking with curiosity on the habitations and movements of the new invaders of their land.

If the stranger now takes his course from the bottom to the upper plain, by way of Broadway, he will see that the city now covers nearly all the upper plain, and the houses begin to ascend the sides, and crown the tops of the hills. But in the days of which we speak, there was scarcely a house in all that region. Alone, and surrounded by a garden and open fields, was the house of WINTHROP SARGENT, Esq., Secretary of the North West Territory, standing on or near what is now Macalister street. On the other side of Broadway, between Third and Fourth, where are now the elegant mansions of Messrs. SHOENBERGER, LAWLER and others, was a corn-field, surrounded by a corn-field fence. Pursuing our way down Fourth street, where now the traveller sees the tallest spire in the United States, and asks "What church is that?" was the first graveyard, where

> "Each in his narrow cell forever laid,
> The rude forefathers of the hamlet slept,"

Not *sleep*, as the poet has it, for in less than a generation since the first rude church was there erected, bones of its founders have either been removed by their surviving relatives, or scattered to the winds by thoughtless strangers! It is but a few years since, when the workmen were digging the cellars of the houses at the North-East corner of Fourth and Walnut streets, large quantities of human bones were disinterred—no friend near to recognize them, and neither stone or history to tell who they were!

The square between Main and Walnut, Fourth and Fifth streets, was originally dedicated as a Public Square. Within

---

* BURNET'S Letters.

FIRST CHURCH BUILT IN CINCINNATI.

the angle of Main and Fourth, where the First Presbyterian Church now stands, was erected the first, and at the time we refer to, the only church of the village of Cincinnati. It was a small frame house, and in rear of it, near Walnut street, stood some years after, a frame school house. In process of time, as this was a "public square," the County Commissioners took possession of the north half, on Fifth street, and there erected a Court House and Jail--both, we believe, made of logs. As time advanced, the school was erected into a college, and finally, the large stone building fronting Walnut street, and occupied by the Mercantile Library Association, and Merchants' Exchange, was built on the school lot. The Public Square thus come into the possession of three corporations--the First Presbyterian Society, the College, and the County Commissioners. The *citizens*, to whom the square properly belonged, lost their rights by non-usance. The County Commissioners removed the Court House, and *leased the lots*; the Church did the same on the Main and Fourth street sides—reserving its own premises on the interior ground; the College built the Walnut street front, and thus, what was intended for a fresh green, pleasant to the tired citizen, has been covered with stores and shops. This *possession* was gradually acquired, so that when the citizens began to wake from their slumber, it was too late to regain their right. A long controversy ensued, which was decided against the city, by lapse of time. In the proceedings, depositions of old settlers were taken, which embody and make permanent the early history of the town.

In the midst of this square, where the old church stood, rises the lofty spire of the new (First Presbyterian) Church, stretching 280 feet into the sky, and offering to such as are able to attain its upper part, a most picturesque and splendid view of the surrounding city.

But we must return to our walk within the ancient village of 1800, which, in the darkness of that profound antiquity, (!) seems to us something like Nineveh, as we endeavor to disinter the mounds, forts, and ancient temples!

As the stranger walks two or three squares further, he will see the slender towers—imitations of the minarets, or some strange architecture—which belongs to the Mechanics' Institute, on the corner of Sixth and Vine streets. This building is on the highest lot of the city, and from the hills seems to stand out in bold relief. "There," says Dr. Drake, "was part of a wheat field of sixteen acres, owned by Mr. James Ferguson, (now living,) fenced in without reference to the streets, which now cut through it. The stubble of that field is still decaying in the soil around the foundations of that noble edifice." In this wheat field, we terminate our wanderings through the Cincinnati of 1800. To the west were mere woods and paths; to the north, Main street was a muddy country road, which soon divided into two—one winding over the hills to Dayton, the other, as now, passing through the valley of Mill-creek, to Hamilton.

On the 4th of July, 1799, the guns of Fort Washington, at morning dawn, poured forth a salute to the last National Anniversary of the 18th century. The troops and militia paraded under Governor St. Clair, and joy, festivities, and sports crowned the day. The Indian conquest was terminated; Fort Washington ceased to be of consequence; the pioneer village began to be a town; and Cincinnati, the Metropolis of the West, began its career of civil and commercial prosperity.

In the fifty years which have intervened between the village and the present city, there were few events which were not in the natural progress of rapid growth, or common to the commercial vicissitudes of the country. There were, however, a few

FIRST PRESBYTERIAN CHURCH, (NEW EDIFICE,) ERECTED 1851-2.

which were peculiar in their character to the natural history of this region, and have become memorable in the annals of the city. The first of these were the EARTHQUAKES of 1811-12. These came upon the inhabitants with great surprise. There were no volcanic mountains within many hundreds of miles, and no such phenomena were known to the early settlers. On the morning of the 16th December, 1811, the inhabitants of Cincinnati and the neighborhood were roused from their beds by a severe shock of earthquake, lasting six or seven minutes, the vibrations of which were from the South West to the North East. On the 23d of January, 1812, was another shock, and on the 7th of February, another, harder than either. In the mean-while, scarcely a day elapsed without evident shaking of the earth. It was ascertained, by an instrument prepared for the purpose, that from December to May there was not a day with-out vibrations. Agitations were felt at subsequent periods, for more than a year, but they gradually wore off, and with the exception of two or three very slight vibrations, have not returned since. The original seat of these earthquakes was near New Madrid, (Mo.) on the Mississippi, where it changed the course of the river, and converted the solid land into pools and lakes.

Some of the shocks at Cincinnati were so violent as to shake down chimneys and partition walls! In WILLIS's Tavern, on Main street, many of the young gentlemen and ladies of the town were boarders. When the first shock came, they rushed into the street as if the Judgment had come, and many a humor-ous story was told at the time—of mammas in their night caps, of papas in their drawers, of maiden beauty unadorned, of bold and slashing soldiers pale with fear—as the motley groupe of old and young were exhibited flying from their beds in the light of a December moon.

In May, 1809, there came through this region, one of those TORNADOES, which in those days were more common than they are now, and were often extremely violent. This wind, like nearly all storms in this valley, commenced in the South West, and by half past 1, P. M. of the 28th, became a whirlwind of prodigious force—sweeping principally over the eastern part of the town. The roof of the "Sargent House," as it was called, standing alone where Macalister street now is, was blown off like a sheet of paper, and caried to the plain below! A new brick school house was blown down; while fences, trees, etc. were uprooted and scattered about in every direction. As the tornado proceeded eastwardly, it made a clear track through the forest, prostrating at once the largest oaks. The road through Lebanon and Wilmington was in many places impassable on account of the labyrinth of trees thrown across it by the tempest. This storm ascended the slope of the Alleghanies, in the afternoon, and in a few hours more passed away to the ocean.

Another memorable event was the Flood of 1832. There have been other "freshets" of the Ohio, as high, or nearly so, as this, but none which was so injurious, or remarkable in its effects. An Indian tradition told of yet higher waters just previous to the arrival of the whites; and in December, 1847, another occurred, within a few inches of the same height. In 1832, however, far more damage was done. The water began to be high on the 7th of February, and continued rapidly rising till the 19th, when it had attained the extraordinary height of sixty-three feet above low water mark! Many frame houses on the banks of the river were floated off, and seen hundreds of miles from the place where built on their way to the Mississippi. Boats were unmoored, men were drowned, animals were destroyed, steamers floated over fields of corn and ran afoul of the forest trees. The river Ohio from the surrounding heights, was as if an ocean had broken over the country, and threatened all the abodes of man. That part of the city near the mouth of Mill-creek, was all submerged; the roofs only of the smaller houses were to be seen, and the taller ones stood like islands in the deep. Steamboats passed up Main to Second street, and the great warehouses on the bottom could be reached only in boats.

This extraordinary "flood" is said to have been caused by the concurrence of three facts, which can rarely happen at the same time. In the first place, the ground was frozen, so that the water could not be absorbed by the earth; then the heavy snows of the mountains melted; and lastly, an immense quantity of rain fell at the same time. A vast amount of water thus accumulated, which, instead of sinking into the earth, was rolled off into the Ohio and its tributaries. The ordinary spring floods of the Ohio do not reach any part of Cincinnati; and it is only once in about twenty years that these great floods may be anticipated.

The next memorable event in the history of Cincinnati was the invasion of the CHOLERA. This was indeed common to nearly all the cities and towns of the country, but there were few which have been visited so severely, or so frequently. The severity of this epidemic here, serves to prove how great and permanent are those causes of growth and prosperity, which have been able not only to overcome such disasters, but in a very brief period to wipe away all traces of their existence. The first visit of the Cholera was in September, 1832, which contined till the first of December following; its greatest violence being in October. In 1833, it returned with less force, and again in the summer of 1834. In these three seasons, about 1500 persons perished with that disease, the population being about 30,000; the mortality by cholera was 1 in 20. In 1849, seventeen years after its first invasion, this destroyer returned again, and with great violence; its prevalence in that season, was chiefly among the foreign immigrants; the Germans and Irish. In 1850, it again returned, and in 1851, slightly, making in all six years, since 1832, in which the cholera has been present. In the three last seasons, about 7,000 died of cholera, making a little more than 1 in 20, or very near the same ratio as before. With the exception of cholera, which has pervaded all countries, and in some much more fatally, Cincinnati has been remarkably healthy, having, strictly speaking, no epidemic of any kind; fever is not common, and consumption not so frequent as in the Eastern States.

The Earthquake, the Tornado, the Flood, the Cholera, were all but temporary disturbances in the course of nature. The first occurred but once in half a century, the second but twice, and the two last appear but casual visitations of Providence. In the meanwhile the village has grown into a town; the town into a city, with a suddenness, a power, and a prosperity, which have no precedent even in this prosperous country.

THE LICKING RIVER—we have spoken of as the war path of the Shawanese. This stream has been remarkable for as many Indian battles, and scenes of danger and adventure as any other locality in the Ohio valley. DANIEL BOONE, the first settler of

Kentucky, was the first white man whose enterprise has signalized the Licking in history. It was in February, 1778, while engaged with a party in making salt, that the bold pioneer was captured by the Indians. They took him to Old Chil-li-co-the, on the Little Miami, just above the present Xenia, thence they took him to Detroit, with a view of selling him (for ransom) to the English; but his captors finally concluded to keep him, his virtues having fairly gained their affections. The following account of Boone and his escape is given in the Western Annals:

"No man could have been better calculated than Boone to disarm the suspicions of the Red Men. Some have called him a white Indian, and except that he never showed the Indian's blood-thirstiness when excited, he was more akin in his loves, his ways, his instincts, his joys, and hissorrows, to the aboriginal inhabitants of the West, than to the Anglo-Saxon invaders. Scarce any other white possessed in an equal degree the true Indian gravity, which comes neither from thought, feeling, or vacuity, but from a bump peculiar to their own craniums. And so in hunting, shooting, and swimming, and other Shawanese amusements, the newly made Indian boy, Boone, spent the month of May, necessity making all the little inconveniences of his lot quite endurable.

"On the 1st of June, his aid was required in the business of salt-making, and for that purpose he and his brethren started for the valley of the Scioto, where he stayed ten days, hunting, boiling brine, and cooking; then the homeward path was taken again. But when Chillicothe was once more reached, a sad sight met our friend Daniel's eyes; four hundred and fifty of the choice warriors of the West, painted in the most exquisite war style, and armed for the battle. He scarce needed to ask whither they were bound; his heart told him Boonesborough; and already, in imagination, he saw the blazing roofs of the little borough he had founded; and he saw the bleeding forms of his friends. Could he do nothing? He would see; meanwhile be a good Indian, and look all ease and joy. He was a long way from his own white homestead; one hundred and fifty miles at least, and a rough and inhospitable country much of the way between him and it. But he had travelled fast and far, and might again. So, without a word to his fellow prisoners, early in the morning of June 16th, without his breakfast, in the most secret manner, unseen, unheard, he departed. He left his red relatives to mourn his loss, and over hill and valley sped, forty miles a day, for four successive days, and ate but one meal by the way. He found the station wholly unprepared to resist so formidable a body as that which threatened it, and it was a matter of life and death that every muscle should be exerted to get all in readiness for the expected visitors. Rapidly the white men toiled in the summer sun, and through the summer night, to repair and complete the fortifications, and to have all as experience had shown it should be. But still the foe came not, and in a few days another escaped captive brought information of the delay of the expedition in consequence of BOONE's flight. The savages had relied on surprising the stations, and their plans being foiled by their adopted son DANIEL, all their plans were unsettled. This proved the salvation of Boonesborough, and probably all the frontier forts, that the founder of Kentucky was taken captive and remained a captive as long as he did. So often do seeming misfortunes prove, in God's hand, our truest good."

In 1779, an expedition was made by the Licking, to the Indian towns, which failed; and in 1779, a body of 600 Canadians and Indians made an expedition up the Licking. It was in consequence of repeated incursions on the settlements of the Licking, that CLARKE made that successful attack on the Indian towns of the Miamis, which, for a time relieved Kentucky.

"An expedition which had been in the neighborhood of Lexington, where the first permanent improvements were made in April of this year, (1779,) upon its return came to the Ohio near the Licking, at the very time that Colonel RODGERS and Captain BENHAM reached the same point on their way up the river in boats. A few of the Indians were seen by the commander of the little American squadron, near the mouth of the Licking; and supposing himself to be far superior in numbers, he caused seventy of his men to land, intending to surround the savages; in a few moments, however, he found he was himself surrounded, and after a hard fought battle, only twenty or twenty-five, or perhaps even fewer, of the party were left alive. It was in connection with this skirmish that a coincidence occurred which seems to belong rather to a fanciful story than to sober history, and which yet appears to be well authenticated. In the party of whites was Captain ROBERT BENHAM. He was one of those that fell, being shot through both hips, so as to be powerless in his lower limbs; he dragged himself, however, to a tree-top, and there lay concealed from the savages after the contest was over. On the evening of the second day, seeing a raccoon, he shot it, but no sooner was the crack of his rifle heard than he distinguished a human voice, not far distant; supposing it to be some Indian, he reloaded his gun and prepared for defence; but a few moments undeceived him, and he discovered that the person whose voice he had heard was a fellow sufferer, with this difference, however, that both his arms were broken! Here then were the only two survivors of the combat, (except those that had entirely escaped,) with one pair of legs and one pair of arms between them. It will be easily believed that they formed a co-partnership for mutual aid and defence. BENHAM shot the game which his friend drove towards him, and the man with sound legs then kicked it to the spot where he with sound arms sat ready to cook it. To procure water, the one with legs took a hat by the brim in his teeth, and walked into the Licking up to his neck, while the man with arms was to make signals if any boat appeared in sight. In this way they spent about six weeks, when, upon the 27th of November, they were rescued. BENHAM afterwards bought and lived upon the land where the battle took place; his companion, Mr. BUTLER tells us, was, a few years since, still living at Brownsville, Pennsylvania."

CLARKE was a remarkable man, whose memory is yet renowned in the West. His knowledge of Indian character was perfect, while his self-command and courage were unrivalled. The following scene, characteristic of the man, is said to have taken place at Fort Finney, mouth of the Great Miami, and is from a late work by Judge HALL:

"The Indians entered in a disorderly and disrespectful manner; the commissioners, without noticing the disorderly conduct of the other party, or appearing to have discovered their meditated treachery, opened the council in due form. They lighted the peace-pipe, and after drawing a few whiffs, passed it to the chiefs, who received it. Colonel CLARKE then rose to explain the purpose for which the treaty was ordered. With an unembarrassed air, with the tone of one accustomed to command, and an easy assurance of perfect security and self-possession, he stated that the commissioners had been sent to offer peace to the Shawanese; that the President had no wish to continue the war; he had no resentment to gratify; and if the red men desired peace, they could have it on reasonable terms. 'If such be the will of the Shawanese,' he concluded, 'let some of their wise men speak.'

"A chief arose, drew up his tall person to its full height, and assuming a haughty attitude, threw his eye contemptuously over the commissioners and their small retinue, as if to measure their insignificance, in comparison with his own numerous train, and then, stalking to the table, threw upon it two belts of wampum, of different colors—the war and the peace belt.

"'We come here,' he exclaimed, 'to offer you two pieces of wampum; they are of different colors; you know what they mean: you can take which you like!' and turning upon his heel, he resumed his seat.

"The chiefs drew themselves up, in the consciousness of having hurled defiance in the teeth of the white men. They offered an insult to the renowned leader of the Long Knives, to which they knew it would be hard to submit, while they did not suppose he dare resent it. The council-pipe was laid aside, those fierce wild men gazed intently at CLARKE. The Americans saw that the crisis had arrived; they could no longer doubt that the Indians understood the advantage they possessed, and were disposed to use it; and a common sense of danger caused each eye to be turned on the leading commissioner. He sat undisturbed and apparently careless until the chief who had thrown the belts upon the table had taken his seat; then with a small cane which he held in his hand, he reached, as if playfully, towards the war belt, entangled the end of the stick in it, drew it towards him, and then with a switch of the cane threw the belt into the midst of the chiefs. The effect was electric. Every man in the council, of each party, sprang to his feet—the savage with a loud exclamation, 'Hugh!'—the Americans in expectation of a hopeless conflict against overwhelming numbers.—Every hand grasped a weapon.

"CLARKE alone was unawed. The expression of his countenance changed to a ferocious sternness, and his eye flashed, but otherwise he was unmoved. A bitter smile was perceptible on his compressed lips, as he gazed upon that savage band, whose hundred eyes were bent fiercely and in horrid exultation upon him as they stood like a pack of wolves at bay thirsting for blood, and ready to rush upon him whenever one bolder than the rest should commence the attack. It was one of those moments of indecision when the slightest weight thrown into either scale will make it preponderate; a moment in which a bold man, conversant with the secret springs of human action, may seize upon the minds of all around him and sway them at his will.

"Such a man was the intrepid Virginian. He spoke, and there was no one bold enough to gainsay him—none that could return the fierce glance of his eye. Raising his arm and waiving his hand toward the door, he exclaimed: 'Dogs! YOU MAY GO!' The Indians hesitated for a moment, and then rushed tumultuously out of the council room."*

The stranger, who in this sketch we supposed to be looking upon the Cincinnati of 1800, clustered round Fort Washington, and half hid amidst the thick forests of the Miamis, now looks upon the busy, active, populous, animated QUEEN OF THE WEST, resting upon the bosom of the Ohio, spreading out over hill and plain, absorbing the commerce of millions, erecting the laboratories of art, and connecting herself by these rail-cars, with distant States, and attracting the inhabitants of distant lands! Let us suppose this stranger to have actually seen, (as some now living have done,) the *village* of Cincinnati, and returning after half a century, to behold it now. On yonder hill, where WHITE EYES watched from his tree-top the soldiers of Fort Washington, rises the OBSERVATORY, having one of the finest telescopes in the world—standing, in fact, as the "Light House of the Skies." Where the "corn field" was, on Broadway, rise the splendid mansions of taste and wealth. Where the "wheat field" was, on Sixth street, is the Mechanics' Institute, dedicated to knowledge and science; where the village school house was, rises the massy structure which contains the Mercantile Library and the Merchants' Exchange; where the "ponds" were on the bottom, are long ranges of stores, and factories, and founderies. All around are thronged streets, and the loud

* HALL, in Wiley & Putnam's Library.

VIEW OF CINCINNATI IN THE YEAR 1809.

roar of business. The slow and narrow ark has been supplanted on the water by the swift and splendid steamer; the wagon, by the coach; the mud road, by the railway; and in one word, the forest gloom, the wigwam, and the cabin, have, in a few short years, disappeared before the advancing light of a gorgeous and brilliant civilization, soon to be exhibited in yet more striking manifestations.

The traveller may feel curious to know something of the atcual *progress* of Cincinnati, and something of the most interesting *facts* in its present condition. Of these we can give only a bird's eye view, and that in the dry form of statistics, and statements. The growth of Cincinnati, for the last half century, and its *rate* of increase is denoted in the following table:

TABLE OF THE POPULATION AND GROWTH OF CINCINNATI WITHIN THE CORPORATE LIMITS.

Years.	Population.	Decennial Increase.	Per Cent.
1800	500		
1810	2,320	1,820	360
1820	9,602	7,282	314
1830	24,831	15,229	158
1840	46,338	21,507	87
1850	116,108	69,770	150

Calculating the growth of Cincinnati, both on its *increments* and also its *per centage* of increase, the result will give 236,000 for the population in 1860, and make it the *third* city of the American Union. Looking to all the elements of progress now at work to increase its business and add to its attraction, this estimate is not extravagant.

To the above table of population we add one of the growth of the northern suburbs, or what were the northern suburbs in 1840. Since then, what are now denominated the 11th and 12th Wards have been cut off from Mill-creek township. The comparison of population in the suburbs is as follows, viz:

	In 1840.	In 1850.
Mill Creek Township, - - - -	6,249	6,287
Eleventh Ward, - - - - - -		19,336
Twelfth Ward, - - - - - -		
Total, - - - - - - -	6,249	25,623

This suburb has heretofore increased at the rate of 300 per cent., and, at this rate, there will be in 1860, nearly 100,000 inhabitants north of the city line in 1840! A general idea of the business of Cincinnati may be obtained from the following statistics:

1. Value of Manufactured Articles and Industrial Production	$55,017,000
2. Exports of strictly Domestic Produce	$10,000,000
" of Southern Productions	4,500,000
" of Merchandise and Manufactures	36,500,000
Total	$51,000,000

3. The Imports may be taken as, in general, equal to the exports, or at least but little less.

The Trade of Cincinnati may be estimated in the aggregate, as nearly or quite equal to one hundred millions of dollars.

As an example of the manufacturing industry of this western city, take the following values of some of the leading articles manufactured for general distribution, and not including any of those, such as carpentry, brick-laying, baking, etc., which are only local.

Manufacture of Iron, of all varieties	$5,547,900
Cloth and Clothing	4,427,500
Leather	2,589,650
Wood and Furniture	2,356,890
Grease and Oils	4,545,000
Alcohol and Liquors	4,191,920
Copper and Tin	515,000
Animal Meats	5,895,000
Books and Publications	1,246,540
Cars and Carriages	255,937
Chemicals	226,000
Flour and Feed	1,690,000
Tobacco	931,000
Steamboats	488,000
White Lead	385,000
Miscellaneous	458,000
Total	$35,840,337

These, as the list shows, do not include the value of merely mechanical labor employed in the city.

4. CHURCHES AND RELIGIOUS ESTABLISHMENTS.—About *one-third* of the inhabitants of Cincinnati are Roman Catholics, who have come from Europe, immigrants in this country. Of these, two-thirds are Germans, who have brought their religion and their language with them. Another large body of Germans are Lutherans, more than one-half of whom are Rationalists. *Six* German Lutheran churches are of this description. The Irish are nearly all Roman Catholics. The Welsh (of whom there are three churches,) are Presbyterians and Methodists. The American churches are divided among the usual Protestant denominations. The following table shows the number of churches in each sect, viz:

EPISCOPALIAN, - - - -	5,	ROMAN CATHOLIC, - -	11,
PRESBYTERIAN, (all kinds,)	19,	METHODISTS, (all kinds,)	22,
BAPTISTS, (all kinds,) -	12,	LUTHERAN, (all kinds,)	10,
FRIENDS, - - - - -	2,	GERMAN REFORMED, -	2,
SWEDENBORGIANS, - -	2,	UNITARIANS, - - -	2,
UNIVERSALISTS, - -	2,	UNITED BRETHREN, -	1,
HEBREW SYNAGOGUES, -	4,	SECOND ADVENT, - -	1,

At the present time, the whole number of churches and religious institutions exceeds 100. The proportion between the great divisions of religious persuasion is estimated thus: Protestants, 62 per cent; Roman Catholics, 35 per cent; and Jews, 3 per cent. The number of foreign immigrants is 46 per cent. and of Americans 54 per cent. It follows from these two statements compared, that 8 per cent of the population are *foreign Protestants*, and that the *foreign* Catholics are to the *foreign* Protestants as 35 to 8, and 3 per cent are Jews. Of all the foreign immigrants, therefore, just *three-fourths* are Roman Catholics.

SCHOOLS AND EDUCATION.—Cincinnati has had a high reputation for its elementary schools; so much so that many families have removed to the city from interior counties, solely to enjoy the benefits of the public schools. These schools are *free* and give a good *common education*. There are also many excellent private institutions, and the Roman Catholic churches have a system of parochial schools. In addition to this there are Female Schools, Academies, and Colleges; besides, Commercial Institutes, Orphan Asylums, Libraries, Medical Colleges, Law

Schools, etc. On the whole, there is scarcely any species of instruction which may not be enjoyed at Cincinnati, and at a cheap rate. Cheap boarding for students may also be had, and there are great facilities for the pursuit of education, both for strangers and citizens.

The statistics of Schools, Academies, and Colleges, etc. in Cincinnati, are as follows:

Institutions.	Number.	Teachers.	Pupils.
Public Schools,	19	138	12,240
Parochial Schools,	13	48	4,494
Private Schools,	50	100	2,500
Colleges,	3	15	403
Medical Colleges,	4	20	450
Mercantile Colleges,	4	12	250
Law School,	1	3	40
Theological Schools,	5	7	100
Colored Schools,	3	9	360
Totals,	102	352	20,837

More than twenty thousand youth are there annually instructed in Cincinnati, in various branches of education, and as the time usually allotted to elementary education is much less than that within which the law limits public education, in that period there is a succession of pupils. It is probable that nearly all the youth of Cincinnati are more or less taught in its schools.

Commercial Institutions.—Banks, Insurance Offices, Private Bankers, the Merchants' Exchange, the Mercantile Library Association, Commercial Colleges, and all the associations for the convenience and promotion of commercial interests, which are found in any city, exist also in Cincinnati. The city has been, and is yet deficient in banking capital, in proportion to the wants of trade. As a consequence, money is in active demand, and the rate of interest high. The disadvantage to the commerce of the city is great, but the profits of business, the sale of domestic products, and the flourishing condition of manufactures, have rapidly accumulated the wealth of the city, and there is among the citizens a large class of wealthy men. The value of property exceeds sixty millions of dollars, and the annual accumulation is at least a tenth part of that. Should its present prosperity continue, the wealth of Cincinnati will, in a few years, equal that of New York.

Public and Charitable Institutions.—A portion of these we have already mentioned. There are others of a protective and charitable nature, in which a stranger will feel interested.

The House of Refuge is one of these. This is about two miles out of the city, and is an institution for the reclamation of youth, of both sexes, who are either viciously inclined, have committed small crimes, or are in dangerous ways, without friends. It is an interesting place, and worth a visit.

The Commercial Hospital, was originally intended for boatmen, for whom an allowance is made by Government; but has gradually become a depository of all the sick poor, who, having no other shelter, are here cared for by the Township Trustees. In consequence of the deficiency of Lunatic Asylums, about 120 lunatics are annually maintained in the Hospital. Women, also, are taken there to lie-in. Patients of all other kinds are also taken there, especially strangers. More than three thousand persons are provided for annually, in this institution.

The Widow's Home, on Mount Auburn, is a new charity, instituted originally as a home for respectable and aged females. The building has just been erected, and it promises to be useful and beneficent.

The Orphan Asylums are five in number and contain four hundred inmates. One is American Protestant, one German Protestant, one Colored, and two Roman Catholic.

The Hotel for Invalids is a private institution for the reception of patients, who having no home, and unwilling to go to the hospital, may here have comfortable attendance and physicians, in comparative retirement.

Temperance, Masonic, and Odd-Fellows Societies are numerous, and have large halls in different parts of the city.

A stranger, who visits Cincinnati, may, if he pleases, find much to interest and occupy him. If he desires to read in quiet and comfort, few places in the United States afford a better selection of either books or newspapers, than may be found in the beautiful library room of the Mercantile Library Association, Walnut, between Fourth and Fifth streets. If he loves the Fine Arts, the Galleries of Paintings, of which there are two, will amuse him for a few hours, and he may also step into the studios of several who are no mean Artists. If he loves Music, there is scarcely an evening without a concert. If he would attend church, there are those of all denominations, who will make him welcome to a seat. Finally, if he be a lover of scenery, and the beauties of nature, he has only to walk or ride over the neighboring hills to behold the most charming views, and delight his eye with the most varied landscapes. From Mount Adams, where the Observatory stands sentinel of the skies; or Mount Auburn, where picturesque gardens and sloping hills are all around, or on the Vine street summits; or over the hills of Mill-creek; or of Kentucky, beyond the river; every where, and all around, the environs of Cincinnati are filled with beautiful and picturesque scenes. In this respect, there is scarcely a town in the United States which equals it. The graceful curves of the surrounding hills, and the gentle windings of the Ohio have supplied the elements of great loveliness in scenery. Travelers from Europe and America have been alike delighted with the aspects of Nature and Art, presented by the environs of Cincinnati. The stranger, who remains more than a day, will scarcely be just to himself who does not take an opportunity to ride over the hills and villages which surround the plain of the city.

St. Peter's Cathedral, on Plum street, between Seventh and Eighth streets, is one of the most beautiful and imposing buildings in the Western country. It is built in the most chaste style of Grecian architecture. Its lofty spire rises 275 feet in height, and its base is a fine portico and colonade. In the rear is the home of Archbishop Purcell and his subordinate Priests. It is built of gray limestone, and has an appearance of both solidity and grandeur.

Having now dwelt for a time on the village of 1800, as well as the city of the present, and glanced at some of its events, its history, and reminiscences, we must bid farewell to the Queen of the West, and hasten with our traveler up the Valley of the Miami.

ST. PETER'S CATHEDRAL.

LITTLE MIAMI RAILROAD.—We are now about to start for Cleveland. The Queen City is behind us. The Forest City is before us. One is on the banks of the beautiful Ohio, the other on the shores of the beautiful Lake. Both were but yesterday covered by the dark and shadowy forest. To-day, one is the Metropolis of the West, and the other a bright and prosperous city, amidst a smiling land! How mutable is every thing in these changing scenes of Time! We are now in the Golden Age. We are bringing out picture after picture, in the brilliant colors of civilization. But, how brief a space since the red Shawanee sat under the lofty oaks upon these hills; and how brief may be the time, in which we shall reach the premature old age of declining empire! Never mind—its our business as good travellers, not to settle the destinies of the world, or to moralize on its changes, but to make ourselves comfortable, and enjoy the scene. There is much to enjoy. We shall cross the whole of Ohio, and see its three largest towns, with forest and field, waving corn, green grass, country farm houses, town boxes, and railway stations. All this we must do in thirteen hours! Only think of it. Two hundred and fifty-four miles in thirteen hours! There goes the whistle!

Before we take note of anything else, let us consider how we are going. The LITTLE MIAMI RAILWAY is the first railway made west of the mountains, and therefore deserves a little notice. It was in the year 1836, that several public spirited gentlemen, of Cincinnati, planned a system of Railroads from Lake Erie to Charleston, South Carolina—a grand chain, which now wants but one link in Kentucky to complete it. At that time the Legislature of Ohio granted a charter for the Mad River Railroad from Sandusky to Dayton, through Springfield. They also granted a charter for a Railroad from Cincinnati to Springfield, to connect with that, called the Little Miami Railroad, because it follows for nearly the whole distance the valley of that stream. The first survey of the road was made by Professor O. M. MITCHEL, whose report was entirely satisfactory. The financial storm, however, prevented even its commencement, till after the law of 1837–38, lending the credit of the State to railroad companies, gave it a new impulse. In 1839, an estimate of its cost was made by R. M. SHOEMAKER, Engineer. And, soon afterwards, the work was commenced. In 1841, the first fourteen miles, to Milford, was completed, and the running of railway cars out of Cincinnati, was deemed one of the wonders of the day. To be suie, the rails being the old flat bar, the cars bounded about as if they were a stage coach. But, there was the smoking locomotive, and the wonder was really accomplished! In three or four more years, the entire line was finished; but not till 1851 was the T Rail fully laid, and the Little Miami Railroad made complete in all its parts. It had thus taken *fourteen years* to finish a railway of eighty-four miles in length, in a State where more miles of Railway are now made or making, than in any State of the Union. At about *twenty-four years* from the first settlement of Cincinnati, the first steamboat commenced running. In about *forty years,* the first turnpike was made, and in *fifty-two years,* the first locomotive began to run!

The Little Miami Railway is now united with the Xenia and Columbus Railway, so that both lines are run, as one, from Cinncinnati to Columbus. The following statistics will give an idea of the principal business features of the work:

L. M. Railroad,		Cincinnati to Xenia	64½	miles.
"	"	Xenia to Springfield	19	"
"	"	Xenia to Columbus	54	"
"	"	Cincinnati to Springfield	83½	"
"	"	Cincinnati to Columbus	118½	"

We are about to take the Columbus route indicated in the last distance.

The actual cost of construction to Springfield	$2,289,000
Actual Receipts in 1851	487,000
Expenses of Running, &c	190,000
Net Proceeds	297,000
Actual Profit on Actual Construction, 13 per cent.	
As, however, $1,100,000 of the cost was loans, at 6 per cent., making the interest	66,000

The *actual profits on the stock* of $1,189,000 was 19 per cent.

There is probably no Railroad in the United States which has yielded a larger profit than this.

The Freight Depot, on the left, is a very large one, being about 300 feet in length; and so great is the business of the Road, that it must soon be enlarged. The Passenger Depot is not yet built, the one we are in being merely a temporary shed.

CINCINNATI WATER WORKS.—On our right, pouring forth its dark smoke, is the Steam Machinery, Forcing Pumps, &c., of the Cincinnati Water Works.

The following are the principal elements of interest in the operations of the Water Works:

Three Steam Engines, with Forcing Pumps, which force into the Reservoir above 5,000,000 gallons in 12 hours.

Reservoir—368 feet long, 135 feet wide, and 23 feet deep.

Capacity of Reservoir	5,000,000	gallons.
Daily Water Consumption of City	2,300,000	"
Iron Pipe	50	miles.
Hydrants	7,000	
Cost of Water Works	$800,000	
Income	75,000	

The Reservoir is on the hill side, just to the left, built of immense walls of limestone. Iron pipes, of various sizes, carry the water to every part of the city. It will be observed that the Reservoir contains about double the supply required for daily consumption, and the working power of the pumps is competent to keep it full. Hence there is the most ample supply for fires and all extra demands.

These two views, the one looking up the river, showing Jamestown, on the Kentucky side of the river, are as beautiful as can be any where seen by the traveller, in early morn. In the view of Jamestown, we see Mt. Tusculum, in the distance. The other view, looking towards the city, is fully equal to this.

JAMESTOWN.

Jamestown is a little Village, about three miles from the Depot, on a projecting curve of the Kentucky shore. It was commenced, but three years since, and has now probably a thousand inhabitants. This is thought by most persons to be one of the most beautiful bends on the Ohio River. The town looks bright and new, while all around it are green lawns, and wood-crowned hills. The Ohio continues its curve to the south for several miles, making rather more than a semicircle; so that from twelve miles above Cincinnati is only six miles in a direct line.

Pendleton and the Car Depots.—Three or four years since, the Company found it necessary to erect extensive depots and workshops, out of the city, and they are seen on the left hand. There are the most ample accommodations for this purpose built in the most substantial manner. The town around is really Fulton, a corporate suburb of Cincinnati; but the new village, built below the Depot, is called Pendleton, from a distinguished citizen of Cincinnati.

VIEW OF THE CAR HOUSES AT PENDLETON. (See page 46.)

JOHN SMITH is a celebrated character in all parts of the world; but he to whom we allude, was Senator from Ohio, in 1803–6, and in some mysterious way, became involved in the ill-fame of Burr's conspiracy. He was an eminent citizen of the North Western Territory, and extensively engaged in mercantile business. His home was on the side hill near where we are.

TUSCULUM is on the hill side and top, just to our left, as we turn into the valley of the Miami. The traveller will see it inclosed with heavy stone walls, some vineyards, and extensive peach orchards. In good years (which is but one in three) the Cincinnati market gets some of its finest fruit from this orchard. The property belongs to Nicholas Longworth, Esq., who has reclaimed the land from barrenness and made it fruitful. The top of this hill has been visited by vast numbers of citizens and foreign travellers. The many and extensive curves which the Ohio river makes, vary and beautify the scenery. From the foot of Tusculum, we see the commencement of the bottoms of the Little Miami, and looking towards the city, we have many views of Fulton and Cincinnati, as seen over the point of the Kentucky plains. To the right, on the point of the hill, we see, on Mount Adams, the Observatory, the corner stone of which was laid by John Quincy Adams, in 1843, on his first and only visit to this section of the West. This is one of the many views which may be seen, as the cars progress between the City and Pendleton Depot, where the train is hitched to the fast locomotive, a distance of three miles.

VIEW OF FULTON, FROM MOUNT TUSCULUM.

Old Columbia was on the bank of the river to our right, as our track curves to the left. There was the *first* settlement of Cincinnati. There the great city was intended to be, but is not. Some new houses are springing up, however, and it will soon be a suburb, and really a part of Cincinnati.

The Columbia settlement was made by Mr. Stites and twenty-six other persons, on the 18th of November, 1788. They built a block-house, named the town Columbia, and prepared for a winter of want and hard fighting. But they were agreeably disappointed. The Indians proved friendly, and they got along very well together. But a new and unexpected enemy arose, which terminated the hopes of a city at Columbia. This was the flood. The water rose so high in January, 1789, that but one house escaped the deluge. The soldiers were obliged to take refuge in the loft of the block-house, and finally in a boat. That flood destroyed the hopes of making the City of Ohio Valley at Marietta, Columbia, or North Bend, and determined its position at Cincinnati. Since the city has almost reached Columbia' it has begun to grow, and, as it is only under water at very high floods, it will probably become a flourishing suburb.

The Old Baptist Burying Ground, appears on a rising knoll, just to the right, as we have fairly turned the hill. This is the oldest burying ground in the Miami country. The following account of the settlement and the burying ground is given by the late Oliver M. Spencer, who was there as early as in 1790.

" It is, perhaps, unknown to many, that the broad and extensive plain stretching along the Ohio from the Crawfish to the mouth, and for three miles up the Little Miami, and now divided into farms, highly cultivated, was the ancient site of Columbia, a town laid out by Major Benjamin Stites, its original proprietor; and by him and others was expected to become a large city, the great capital of the West. From Crawfish, the small creek forming its north-western boundary, more than one mile up the Ohio, and extending back about three-fourths of a mile, and half way up the high hill which formed a part of its eastern and northern limits, the ground was laid off into blocks, containing each eight lots of half an acre, bounded by streets intersected at right angles. The residue of the plain was divided into lots of four and five acres, for the accommodation of the town. Over this plain, on our arrival, we found scattered, about fifty cabins, flanked by a small stockade nearly half a mile below the mouth of the Miami, together with a few block-houses for the protection of the inhabitants, at suitable distances along the bank of the Ohio.

"Fresh in my remembrance is the rude log-house, the first humble sanctuary of the first settlers of Columbia, standing amidst the tall forest trees, on the beautiful knoll, where now (1834) is a grave-yard, and the ruins of a Baptist meeting-house of later years. There, on the holy Sabbath, we were wont to assemble to hear the word of life; but our fathers met with their muskets and rifles, prepared for action, and ready to repel any attack of the enemy. And while the watchman on the walls of Zion was uttering his faithful and pathetic warning, the sentinels without, at a few rods' distance, with measured step, were now pacing their walks, and now standing, and with strained eyes endeavoring to pierce through the distance, carefully scanning every object that seemed to have life or motion.

The first clergyman I there heard preach was Mr. GANO, father of the late General GANO, of this city, then a captain, and one of the earliest settlers of Columbia. Never shall I forget that holy and venerable man, with locks white with years, as with a voice tremulous with age, he ably expounded the word of truth.

"I well recollect, that in 1791, so scarce and dear was flour, that the little that could be afforded in families, was laid by to be used only in sickness, or for the entertainment of friends, and although corn was then abundant, there was but one mill, (WICKERHAM'S) a floating mill, on the Little Miami, near where TURPIN'S now (1834) stands: it was built in a small flatboat, tied to the bank, its wheel turning slowly with the natural current running between the flat and a small pirogue anchored in the stream, and on which one end of its shaft rested; and having only one pair of small stones, it was at best barely sufficient to supply meal for the inhabitants of Columbia and the neighboring families; and sometimes from low water and other unfavorable circumstances, it was of little use, so that we were obliged to supply the deficiency from hand-mills, a most laborious mode of grinding.

"The winter of 1791–2 was followed by an early and delightful spring; indeed, I have often thought that our first western winters were much milder, our springs earlier, and our autumns longer than they now are. On the last of February, some of the trees were putting forth their foliage; in March, the red-bud, the hawthorn, and the dog-wood, in full bloom, checkered the hills, displaying their beautiful colors of rose and lily, and in April, the ground was covered with May apple, bloodroot, ginseng, violets, and a great variety of herbs and flowers. Flocks of paroquets were seen, decked in their rich plumage of green and gold. Birds of various species, and of every hue, were flitting from tree to tree, and the beautiful redbird, and the untaught songsters of the West, made the woods vocal with their melody. Now might be heard the plaintive wail of the dove, and now the rumbling drum of the partridge, or the loud gobble of the turkey. Here might be seen the clumsy bear, doggedly moving off, or urged by pursuit into a labored gallop, retreating to his citadel in the top of some lofty tree; or approached suddenly, raising himself erect in the attitude of defence, facing his enemy and waiting his approach; there the timid deer, watchfully resting, or cautiously feeding, or aroused from his thicket, gracefully bounding off, then stopping, erecting his stately head and for a moment gazing around, or snuffing the air to ascertain his enemy, instantly springing off, clearing logs and bushes at a bound, and soon distancing his pursuers. It seemed an earthly paradise; and but for apprehension of the wily copperhead, who lay silently coiled among the leaves, or beneath the plants, waiting to strike his victim; the horrid rattlesnake, who, more chivalrous, however, with head erect amidst its ample folds, prepared to dart upon his foe, generously with the loud noise of his rattle, apprised him of danger; and the still more fearful and insidious savage, who, crawling upon the ground, or noiselessly approaching beyond trees and thickets, sped the deadly shaft or fatal bullet, you might have fancied you were in the confines of Eden, or the borders of Elysium.

"At this delightful season, the inhabitants of our village went forth to their labor, inclosing their fields, which the spring flood had opened, tilling their ground, and planting their corn for the next year's sustenance. I said, went forth, for their principal corn-field was distant from Columbia about one and a half miles east, and adjoining the extensive plain on which the town stood. That large tract of alluvial ground, still known by the name of Turkey Bottom, and which, lying about fifteen feet below the adjoining plain, and annually overflowed, is yet very fertile, was laid off into lots of five acres each, and owned by the inhabitants of Columbia; some possessing one, and others two or more lots; and to save labor was enclosed with one fence. Here the men generally worked in companies, exchanging labor, or in adjoining fields, with their fire-arms near them, that in case of an attack they might be ready to unite for their common defence. Here, their usual annual crop of corn, from ground very ordinarily cultivated, was eighty bushels per acre, and some lots, well tilled, produced one hundred, and in very favorable seasons, a hundred and ten bushels to the acre. An inhabitant of New England, New Jersey, or some portions of Maryland, would scarcely think it credible, that in hills four feet apart, were four or five stalks, one and a half inches in diameter, and fifteen feet in height, bearing each two or three ears of corn, of which some were so far from the ground, that to pull them, an ordinary man was obliged to stand on tiptoe."

NEWTOWN.--Eight miles from Cincinnati, across the Miami, and just visible through the trees, is the village of Newtown, a small town, amidst the wide cornfields of the Miamis. Two or three miles beyond that, as the workmen were cutting a turnpike road through the edge of a small hill, or mound, they disinterred a large quantity of human bones. They were the skulls and bones of hundreds of men, indicating, doubtless, that there had been a great battle between some of the Indian tribes.

PLAINVILLE, 10 miles from Cincinnati, 54 from Xenia, is only a station. A tavern, car factory, station house, and one or two dwellings make up the place.

ROUND BOTTOM—12 miles from Cincinnati, is so called from its being in a circular form, and spreading out, making an extensive bottom. It was long planted only in Indian corn. It may be seen to the right.

MILFORD, 14 miles from Cincinnati, and 50 from Xenia, is a very handsome rural town, on the banks of the Miami, as seen in this view coming towards Cincinnati. The scene here is quite picturesque, and well worth observing. Beyond the river to the south lies the town, with mill and churches in sight, and green hills rising beyond it. Near you is the river, and a bridge, over which a turnpike road leads to the town, and country beyond. A stage is waiting to receive passengers. The station and half dozen houses this side the river, is called Montauk. On your north are hills, and beyond, as you will see, in passing, the Railway goes along the banks of the river. All in all, this is as pleasant a scene, combining town and country, as we shall see.

Clermont County.—Milford is in one edge of Clermont county; and, as we shall pass (after crossing the Miami) a short distance in it, we may as well look at its characteristics now. Clermont is well watered by the East fork of the Little Miami, and its tributary streams. On the south side it has a boundary on the Ohio river, of twenty-five miles, and contains numerous villages and fertile lands. Its statistics are as follows:

Surface	450 square miles.
Acres	288,000 acres.
Production of Corn, estimated	1,500,000 bushels.
Production of Wheat	500,000 "
Cattle,	11,127
Horses	7,969
Swine	38,477
Assessed Value of Property	$6,852,594
Population	30,500
Average Value to a Family of Six Persons	$1,375

There is not so much bottom land in this county as in some we shall see; nor is there as good a cultivation in all parts. Yet, taken as a whole, Clermont is a fertile and prosperous county.

Little Miami River—Bridge—18 miles from Cincinnati, 46 from Xenia. Since leaving Columbia, for the last twelve miles, we have been moving along the banks of the Miami. This stream is rapid in its course, very winding, and is yet shaded, for most of the way, with native trees. The farmers in this country seldom cultivate lands down to the water's edge.

The consequence is, there are few green swards on the river banks, and they generally appear ragged and bushy.

The Little Miami rises in the southwest part of the county of Madison, turns to the north, and after traversing portions of the counties of Clark, Greene, Warren, Clermont, and Hamilton, joins the Ohio, seven miles above Cincinnati. It is a remarkably useful stream, having on its waters upwards of sixty mills, besides other factories. We shall now make its acquaintance, for nearly its whole extent. We here cross it on a bridge, and the stream must be looked for on the left hand.

Loveland's—23 miles from Cincinnati, and 41½ from Xenia, is a new village at the mouth of O'Bannion creek and the junction of the Hillsborough Railroad. As it is eight or ten miles from other towns on the Railroad, it will probably make quite a flourishing village.

THE HILLSBOROUGH RAILROAD branches off here, and goes to the thriving town of Hillsborough, the county seat of Highland county. The road is 37 miles in length, passing through Blanchester and Lynchburgh. Highland is one of the best grain counties of the State, and an extensive railroad business is already commenced. The Hillsborough Company has a charter to extend its road eastwardly to the Ohio river, and surveys of the route have already been made.

WARREN COUNTY LINE.—After passing O'Bannion creek, we are in the county of Warren, a rich and fertile county, having much that is interesting, both in its material and its *personnel*. At present we will sketch its physical features. Warren is the only county, except Hamilton, which is in the valleys of both the Great and Little Miamis. While its main body is intersected by the Little Miami, one corner of it, at the town of Franklin, lies on the Great Miami. The former stream flows through it for thirty-five miles. In addition, its tributaries, Todd's Fork and Cannon's creek flow through the eastern part of the county; so that there are few bodies of land, of the same extent, which are so well watered, and afford such extensive corn bottoms. The following are the statistics of Warren, for 1851:

Surface	400 square miles.
Acres of Land	256,000

Acres cultivated in Corn	42,322	
Production of Corn	1,757,409	bushels.
Average Crop of Corn, per acre	43	"
Acres cultivated in Wheat	25,990	
Production of Wheat	447,042	"
Average Crop of Wheat per acre	17½	"
Number of Horses	8,313	
" of Cattle	12,340	
" of Swine	28,305	
" of Sheep	21,658	
Assessed Value of Property	$8,303,324	
Average Value of Property for each Family of 6 persons	$1,666	

In the northern parts of Warren are extensive settlements of Quakers, and these with Jerseymen and their descendants, make up the largest part of the inhabitants. There are many thriving towns in this county, of which Lebanon, Waynesville, Franklin, Morrow, Deerfield, and Mason are the chief.

MORROW HOUSE AND MILL—26 miles from Cincinnati, 38½ from Xenia. If the traveller will, after reaching 25 miles from Cincinnati, keep a watch on the opposite bank of the river to the left, he will see a large flour mill, and just above it a plain, frame, unpainted house, standing amidst trees, with the hills back, and perhaps half a mile beyond, a bridge, which appears in the distance. This plain, frame house should be regarded, by the passing traveller, with as much veneration, as if it had been the home of a HAMPDEN, a HENRY, or a MADISON; for here lived, during near half a century, one of the most upright, disinterested, useful, and yet unpretending statesmen of our country; one of those who laid deep and solid the foundations of our Republican greatness.

JEREMIAH MORROW was born in Pennsylvania, about the commencement of the Revolutionary war, and settled in the Miami country about 1798–9. He died in 1852, having been for half a century one of the most eminent, and useful men in the State and nation.

In November, 1802, he was a member of the State Convention, from the then county of Hamilton. The Convention was composed of thirty-five members, from nine counties, (there are now eighty-seven), and the Constitution was made in thirty days. It was the most entirely free, liberal, unrestrictive instrument, at the time, in the United States. It remained till 1851, when the innovating spirit of the age changed it for one which is certainly no better. In 1803, MORROW was elected to Congress, in the House of Representatives, where he remained till 1813, the *sole* Representative from the State of Ohio, which has now twenty-one Representatives in that House. In 1813, MORROW took his seat in the United States Senate, where he continued till 1819. In 1822, MORROW was elected Governor of Ohio; re-elected in 1824, and terminated his office by constitutional limitation, in 1826. In the year 1828, the Miami Canal was commenced, and a celebration took place, at Middletown, at which Governor MORROW, Governor CLINTON, of New York, and other gentlemen attended. We well remember seeing the stalwart arm of MORROW strike the first spade into the earth. He was no holiday man, but one of the rugged farmers of the land.

In 1841, MORROW was again elected to the House of Representatives, and finally left Congress in 1843. At that time, he became President of the Little Miami Railroad Company, and remained so till its completion. His last public office was that of President of The Society for the Education of Female Teachers. It will be seen that MORROW was twenty years in Congress, four years Governor, several years President of the Railroad Company, besides performing many other important public functions. In fine, it may be said, that MORROW was all his life one of the Elders of the Republic; a granite pillar, in the social and political edifice. His manners were plain, his person of middle height and of strong, rugged features; his character was remarkable for its uprightness, simplicity, and purity. He was a man of piety, of patriotism, of good will, and of good works. Such was one of the founders of Ohio; and yonder, in that plain, unpretending mansion did he long live under the native oaks, and on the green turf of the Miami.

In 1825, (while Governor,) MORROW was visited by his Highness the Duke of Saxe Weimar, who gives the following account of him and his mansion:

"The dwelling of the Governor consists of a plain frame house, situated on a little elevation not far from the shore of the Little Miami, and is entirely surrounded by fields. The business of the State calls him once a month to Columbus, the seat of government, and the remainder of his time he passes at his country seat, occupied with farming, a faithful copy of an ancient Cincinnatus; he was engaged at our arrival in cutting a wagon pole, but he immediately stopped his work to give us a hearty welcome. He appeared to be about fifty years of age; is not tall, but thin and strong, and has an expressive physiognomy, with dark and animated eyes. He is a native of Pennsylvania, and was one of the first settlers in the State of Ohio. He offered us a night's lodging at his house, which invitation we accepted very thankfully. When seated round the chimney fire in the evening, he related to us a great many of the dangers and difficulties the first settlers had to contend with. We spent our evening with the Governor and his lady. Their children are settled, and they have with them only a couple of grandchildren. When we took our seats at supper, the Governor made a prayer. There was a Bible and several religious books lying on the table. After breakfasting with our hospitable host we took our leave."

Foster's Crossings—26½ miles from Cincinnati, and 38 miles from Xenia. This is only a station, but one which affords quite a pretty little view. To the left is a bridge over the Miami, and a turnpike road, leading up the hill beyond. Near by is a large brick tavern, and the river rolls along brightly and pleasantly. It is called "Crossings," because here the Montgomery turnpike, which we see to the left, crosses the river and the railway.

DEERFIELD--32 miles from Cincinnati, and 32½ from Xenia, is, for a new county, rather an old town. It was laid out in 1795, and for a long time was a frontier town. In consequence of being on low ground, subject to inundation, Deerfield has not flourished much. It is seen on the opposite side of the river, and is connected with the station by a bridge.

This is the station for the LEBANON passengers, for whom a coach is in waiting. Lebanon is the county seat of Warren county, a smart town of near 2,000 inhabitants. It was settled but a short time after Deerfield.

Among the early settlers was Capt. ROBERT BENHAM. He lived in a double cabin, about a mile below Lebanon, on what is now known as the Fearney farm, where he died a few years previous to the late war. He was one of a party of seventy men, who were attacked by Indians near the Ohio, opposite Cincinnati, in the war of the Revolution, the circumstances of which here follow from a published source:

"In the autumn of 1779, a number of keel boats were ascending the Ohio under the command of Maj. RODGERS, and had advanced as far as the mouth of Licking without accident. Here, however, they observed a few Indians standing upon the extremity of a sandbar, while a canoe, rowed by three others, was in the act of putting off from the Kentucky shore, as if for the purpose of taking them aboard. RODGERS immediately ordered the boats to be made fast on the Kentucky shore, while the crew, to the number of seventy men, well armed, cautiously advanced in such a manner as to encircle the spot where the enemy had been seen to land. Only five or six Indians had been seen, and no one dreamed of encountering more than fifteen or twenty enemies. When RODGERS, however, had, as he supposed, completely surrounded the enemy, and was preparing to rush upon them, from several quarters at once he was thunderstruck at beholding several hundred savages suddenly spring up in front, rear, and upon both flanks! They instantly poured in a close discharge of rifles, and throwing down their guns, fell upon the survivors with the tomahawk! The panic was complete, and the slaughter prodigious. Major RODGERS, together with forty-five others of his men, were quickly destroyed. The survivors made an effort to regain their boats, but the five men who had been left in charge of them, had immediately put off from shore in the hindmost boat, and the enemy had already gained possession of the others. Disappointed in the attempt, they turned furiously upon the enemy, and aided by the approach of darkness, forced their way through their lines, and with the loss of several severely wounded, at length effected their escape to Harrodsburgh.

"Among the wounded was Captain ROBERT BENHAM. Shortly after breaking through the enemy's line, he was shot through both hips, and the bones being shattered, he fell to the ground. Fortunately a large tree had lately fallen near the spot where he lay, and, with great pain he dragged himself into the top, and lay concealed among the branches. The Indians, eager in pursuit of the others, passed him without notice, and by midnight all was quiet. On the following day, the Indians returned to the battle ground, in order to strip the dead and take care of the boats. BENHAM, although in danger of famishing, permitted them to pass without making known his condition, very correctly supposing that his crippled legs would only induce them to tomahawk him upon the spot, in order to avoid the trouble of carrying him to their town. He lay close, therefore, until the evening of the second day, when perceiving a raccoon descending a tree, near him, he shot it, hoping to devise some means of reaching it, when he could kindle a fire and make a meal. Scarcely had his gun cracked, however, when he heard a human cry, apparently not more than fifty yards off. Supposing it to be an Indian, he hastily reloaded his gun, and remained silent, expecting the approach of an enemy. Presently the same voice was heard again, but much nearer. Still BENHAM made no reply, but cocked his gun and sat ready to fire as soon as an object appeared. A third halloo was quickly heard, followed by an exclamation of impatience and distress, which convinced BENHAM that the unknown must be a Kentuckian. As soon, therefore, as he heard the expression, "whoever you are, for God's sake answer me!" he replied with readiness, and the parties were soon together. BENHAM, as we have already observed, was shot through both legs! the man who now appeared, had escaped from the same battle *with both arms broken!* Thus each was enabled to supply what the other wanted. BENHAM, having the perfect use of his arms, could load his gun and kill game with great readiness, while his friend having the use of his legs, could kick the game to the spot where BENHAM sat, who was thus enabled to cook it. When no wood was near them, his companion would rake up brush with his feet, and gradually roll it within reach of BENHAM's hands, who constantly fed his companion and dressed *his* wounds, as well as his own—tearing up both their shirts for that purpose. They found some difficulty in procuring water at first, but BENHAM, at length, took his own hat, and placing the rim between the teeth of his companion, directed him to wade into the Licking, up to his neck, and dip the hat into the water (by sinking his own head.) The man who could walk, was thus enabled to bring water, by means of his teeth, which BENHAM could afterwards dispose of as was necessary.

"In a few days they had killed all the squirrels and birds within reach, and the man with the broken arms was sent out to drive game within gunshot of the spot to which BENHAM was confined. Fortunately, wild turkeys were abundant in those woods, and his companion would walk around and drive them towards BENHAM, who seldom failed to kill two or three of each flock. In this manner they supported themselves for several weeks, until their wounds had healed, so as to enable them to travel. They then shifted their quarters, and put up a small shed at the mouth of Licking, where they encamped until late in November, anxiously expecting the arrival of some boat, which should convey them to the Falls of the Ohio.

"On the 27th of November, they observed a flatboat moving leisurely down the river. BENHAM hoisted his hat upon a stick and hallooed loudly for help. The crew, however, supposing them to be Indians—at least suspecting them of an intention to decoy them ashore, paid no attention to their signals of distress, but instantly put over to the opposite side of the river, and manning every oar, endeavored to pass them as rapidly as possible. BENHAM beheld them pass with a sensation bordering on despair, for the place was much frequented by Indians, and the approach of winter threatened them with destruction, unless speedily relieved. At length, after the boat had passed him nearly half a mile, he saw a canoe put off from its stern, and cautiously approach the Kentucky shore, evidently reconnoitering them with great suspicion. He called loudly upon them for assistance, mentioned his name and made known his condition.

After a long parley, and many evidences of reluctance on the part of the crew, the canoe at length touched the shore, and BENHAM and his friend were taken on board. Their appearance excited much suspicion. They were almost entirely naked, and their faces were garnished with six weeks' growth of beard. The one was barely able to hobble upon crutches, and the other could manage to feed himself with one of his hands. They were taken to Louisville, where their clothes (which had been carried off in the boat which deserted them) were restored to them, and after a few weeks' confinement, both were perfectly restored.

"BENHAM afterwards served in the northwest throughout the whole of the Indian war—accompanied the expeditions of HARMAR and WILKINSON, shared in the disaster of ST. CLAIR, and afterwards in the triumph of WAYNE."

Warren county, and particularly Lebanon, has been distinguished by some remarkable men who have adorned their country's history. Among these is JOHN McLEAN, now one of the Justices of the Supreme Court of the United States. Judge McLEAN is a native of New Jersey, whence his family emigrated to Kentucky. He came to the Miami country about fifty years since. In 1806, we find him setting up the "Western Star," (still continued,) a political newspaper, in the town of Lebanon. The paper was originally of Jeffersonian politics, and is now Whig. Mr. McLEAN stood high in popular estimation, for, in 1813, we find him elected to Congress, (in the House of Representatives,) where he remained till 1816.

In December, 1823, he was appointed by Mr. MONROE, Post Master General, and was continued by Mr. ADAMS, through his administration. In March, 1829, he was appointed by President JACKSON, one of the Associate Judges of the Supreme Court of the United States, in which important position he has now remained twenty-three years. It is now nearly forty years since JOHN McLEAN entered public life; he has uniformly performed his duties with credit, dignity, and the public satisfaction. He has sustained the character of a pure, upright, and irreproachable man. In his person, Judge McLEAN is tall, well proportioned, with high brow, open countenance, and robust frame. In his private life, he is amiable and excellent; a distinguished member of the Methodist church, and a practical Christian.

The Hon. THOMAS CORWIN, Secretary of the Treasury, is another of the distinguished citizens of Lebanon. He was born, we believe, in Kentucky, but came early to Ohio. By profession a lawyer, and an eloquent one, he was early engaged in politics, and became member of the Legislature nearly thirty-five years since. Since that, he has been, almost all the time, in public life. Elected to Congress, in 1831, from the district composed of the counties of Warren, Clinton, and Highland, he remained in the House of Representatives till 1840. In that year he was elected Governor, in which place he served till 1842, when he was defeated by Mr. SHANNON, in consequence of the unpopularity reflected upon him by the resignation or "absquatulation," as it was popularly termed, of the members of the Legislature. In 1845, he was elected to the United States Senate, where he remained, till 1851. On the death of General TAYLOR, he was appointed Secretary of the Treasury, by Mr. FILLMORE. It was said by many that he was too indolent for an administrative office. But the reverse is the fact. He has proved one of the most industrious public officers ever in place. It is chiefly as an orator, however that he has acquired celebrity. In the style of his eloquence, he is more like SHERIDAN than any one since that time. His speeches are full of wit, humor, irony, and gorgeous descriptions. Whoever will read his speech, delivered in the Senate, on the Mexican war, will find it one of the finest specimens of American eloquence. There are in all our annals but three or four examples of so well sustained and finished orations as that. Mr. CORWIN, it must be remembered, was in a small minority; the great body of politicians and people being for carrying on the war. His speech on Mr. CLAYTON'S Compromise Bill, in reference to Mexican Territory, was also a very complete argument.

Mr. CORWIN is in person tall, stout, and of a dark, swarthy complexion, from which he is called, by the people, "Black Tom." His countenance is capable of the greatest variety of expression, and no man in the United States equals him in the power of gesticulation, and pantomime. In his manner and character, he is social, amiable, courteous, upright and sagacious; a great favorite with his friends, and popular with the people.

The Honorable THOMAS R. ROSS, of Lebanon, was also an able man, who represented his district, in Congress, from 1819 to 1825, and gave one of the two votes in Congress, from this State for JACKSON.

We might pursue this episodical biography farther, but we are confined to the line of the Railroad, and now we are fast leaving the Deerfield station behind.

MORROW—37 miles from Cincinnati and 27½ from Xenia, is just before us. It is a handsome village of some 800 inhabiants, situated at the mouth of Todd's Fork of the Little Miami. Before the Railway came, there was no village at all here, and now, what a thriving village is here! Todd's Fork rises on the table land of Clinton county, and after running some twenty-five miles, becomes a tributary of the Miami at this point.

The cut represents a view one mile below Fort Ancient, where, in order to preserve the curve, the road has been carried near to the middle of the Miami river. The work is well done, and the bank firmly sustained. We have not in this work, or any of the others on this line, any of those bold structures of the architect and engineer, passing over precipices—up mountains, or traversing rapid flowing rivers, such as are seen on the Erie or North River railroads; but we have a continued succession of beautiful views—houses, rich lands, and thriving villages in the prospect, relieved by streams of water turned into active use. From the curve at Columbia, the course of the road to near Xenia winds up along the Little Miami river, and running along the margin of that stream reveals a continued succession of views, which are not surpassed by those on the Mohawk, in New York. The Miami has considerable fall, and at each short distance a slight dam is thrown across to obtain a fall of water for a paper-mill, flour-mill, or other manufactories, which, for their products, find a ready market in Cincinnati. One of the many of these views we give in the annexed cut. The country on either side of this road, and bordering on this river, is beautiful—undulating—luxuriant. The products of agriculture are continually increasing, under the beneficial influence of this road—which by affording a means of speedily obtaining a ready and certain market, has advanced many hundred fold the price of land—added many hundred fold to the number of the population, and is now by reaction, reaping the advantage by continual increase of way freight and passengers.

We give no view of Fort Ancient—an enterprising, improving place. On the opposite side are seen several mills of importance—one of them a paper-mill of unpretending appearance, but which turns out, for the Cincinnati market, a very large amount of paper. Distilleries, where a large amount of grain is turned into whisky, and a large number of hogs are fattened and slaughtered for the Cincinnati market, will be seen. The Little Miami, along the margin of which we will yet run, affords many pleasant retreats from the heat and dust of Cincinnati, and which is improved by many anglers and huntsmen.

FORT ANCIENT—43 miles from Cincinnati, 21½ from Xenia. This is a name given, from one of the most remarkable ancient fortifications in America. Unfortunately the traveller can see nothing of it from the Railway. On the right hand is a public house, with the sign, "Fort Ancient," and behind, a range of quite high hills. The ancient Fort is on a plain, running back from the summits. No engineer of this day can select a position, or arrange the works with more skill, than that was selected and built by its founders. The Miami river was in front, to which ran a rivulet above, and a rivulet below—each with high banks. Between these was built the Fort, with parapets on the river, and the creek; so that the position was really open on only one side—the east—and there it was well fortified. The following description is by CALEB ATWATER, and published in the *Archæologia Americana:*

"The fortification stands on a plain, nearly horizontal, about 236 feet above the level of the river, between two branches, with very steep and deep banks. The openings in the walls are the gateways. The plain extends eastward along the State road, nearly level, about half a mile. The fortification, on all sides, except the east and west, where the road runs, is surrounded with precipices nearly in the shape of the wall. The wall on the inside varies in its height, according to the shape of the ground on the outside, being generally from eight to ten feet; but on the plain, it is about nineteen and a half feet high inside and out, on a base of four and a half poles. In a few places it appears to be washed away in gutters, made by water collecting on the inside.

"At about twenty poles east from the gate, through which the State road runs, are two mounds, about ten feet eight inches high, the road running between them nearly equidistant from each. From these mounds are gutters running nearly north and south, that appear to be artificial, and made to communicate with the branches on each side. Northeast from the mounds, on the plain are two roads, each about one pole wide, elevated about three feet, and which run nearly parallel, about one-fourth of a mile, and then form an irregular semicircle around a small mound. Near the southwest end of the fortification there are three circular roads, between thirty and forty poles in length, cut out of the precipice between the wall and the river. The wall is made of earth.

"Many conjectures have been made as to the design of the authors in erecting a work with no less than 58 gateways. Several of these openings have evidently been occasioned by the water, which had been collected on the inside until it overflowed the walls and wore itself a passage. In several other places the walls might never have been completed.

"The three parallel roads, dug at a great expense of labor, into the rocks and rocky soil adjacent, and parallel to the Little Miami river, appear to have been designed for persons to stand on, who wished to annoy those who were passing up and down the river. The Indians, as I have been informed, made this use of these roads in their wars with each other and with the whites. Whether these works all belong to the same era and the same people, I cannot say, but the general opinion is that they do. On the whole, I have ventured to class them among "Ancient Fortifications," to which they appear to have higher claims than almost any other, for reasons too apparent to require a recital.

"The two parallel lines are two roads very similar to modern turnpikes, and are made to suit the nature of the soil and make of the ground. If the roads were for foot races, the mounds were the goals from whence the pedestrians started, or around which they ran. The area which these parallel walls enclose, smoothed by art, might have been the place where games were celebrated. We cannot say that these works were designed for such purposes; but we can say, that similar works were thus used among the early inhabitants of Greece and Rome."

WAYNESVILLE, FROM CORWIN.

Corwin—50 miles from Cincinnati, and 14½ from Xenia, is the Station for Waynesville, a neat and handsome town, seen to the left, on the bank of the Little Miami. This town and neighborhood is mostly settled by members of the society of Friends, of whom there are many through this section of country. Waynesville has near a thousand inhabitants. It has two Friends' meeting houses, one Methodist church, and several mills and factories.

Greene County Line—54 miles from Cincinnati, and 10½ from Xenia. Greene county, upon which we are now about to enter, is one of the best districts, both in land and population, in the United States. It is healthy, thriving and productive, and inhabited by an intelligent and religious people. It is most admirably watered, having, on the north-west corner, Mad river, through the midst, the Little Miami; in the north-east, Massie's creek, and, on the south-east, Cæsar's creek. The land is high, and generally level, except where it gradually descends to the water courses. It has quarries of marble of a bluish cast, about four miles from Xenia, and the best of limestone, of which immense quantities of lime are made for the Cincinnati market.

The statistics of Greene county are as follows:

Surface	400	square miles.
Acres of surface	256,000	
Acres planted in Corn	33,177	
Corn produced	1,170,543	bushels.
Acres planted in Wheat	28,550	
Wheat produced	576,258	bushels.
Average Corn per acre	33	"
Average Wheat per acre	20½	"
Number of Cattle	12,146	
Number of Horses	7,347	
Number of Sheep	36,661	
Number of Swine	26,907	
Population	21,947	
Assessed Value of Property, real and personal	$7,642,580	
Assessed Value to each Family of six persons	$2,100	

It will be observed, that in proportion to the population, this is a very wealthy county. The amount of grain raised does not fairly express the agricultural production of the county; for much of the land in the eastern section is employed in grazing.

The Gold Mines—56 miles from Cincinnati. In 1851, some black sand, on the farm of Mr. Mosely, was found to contain some glittering particles, which turned out to be *gold!* Soon it was noised about, that there was a gold mine discovered, and quite a number of people were gathered to dig gold. It turned out, however, to be no California. Either the golden sands gave out, or they were not rich enough to pay the laborers. In a short time, the gold and its miners vanished, and we have heard no more of the Gold mines of Greene!

Spring Valley—57 miles from Cincinnati, and seven from Xenia. This pretty little village is called "Spring Valley," on account of the numerous little springs which gush from the side hills. The town is small, but pleasant, one of those quiet, unassuming places that have grown up without any particular reason, except that it is in the midst of a thriving population. The turnpike, from Cincinnati to Xenia, passes through; also, a

turnpike from Bellbrook. The Miami is about half a mile to the left, and is crossed by a bridge. There is in the neighborhood of this place two factories and several mills.

Valley of Glady.—From Spring Valley to Xenia is seven miles, and for six miles the railway follows a little stream called Glady. This stream seems of little consequence, and the traveler would hardly notice it; yet it is put to many uses, and is an important feature in this section of country. Between Xenia and Spring Valley, there are *seven* mills and factories put in operation by this run! In fact the hills through which it runs are full of springs, and these furnish a never failing supply of water to Glady, and by a little ingenuity it is made to turn many wheels.

Xenia.—The pleasant looking town, on the eminence to the left, with its church spires, its green trees, and thrifty appearance, is Xenia, the county seat of Greene county. It is a place of about three thousand inhabitants, having twelve churches, good schools, and intelligent society. This town and county are remarkable for the intelligence, good morals, and good condition of its people. Its early settlers were principally a good class of people, and it has since been extensively recuited from the different denominations of Scotch Presbyterians, called Seceders—Associate Reformed, and Covenanters. Nevertheless, there was in early times a good deal of the rough and tumble of frontier life. Mr. THOMAS COKE WRIGHT, in some sketches of the county, gives the following scenes:

"But to return to the court. From a careful examination of the records and other sources of information, I cannot learn there was any business for the grand jury when they retired. But they were not permitted to remain idle long. The spectators in attendance promptly took the matter into consideration. They, doubtless, thought it a great pity to have a learned court and nothing for it to do: so they set to and cut out employment for their honors, by engaging in divers hard fights and fisty-cuffs, right on the ground. So it seems our pioneers fought for the benefit of the court. At all events, while their honors were waiting to settle differences according to law, they were making up issues and settling them by trial "*by combat*"—a process by which they avoided the much complained of "law's delay," and incurred no other damages than black eyes and bloody noses, which were regarded as mere trifles, of course. Among the incidents of the day, characteristic of the times, was this: A Mr. ——, from Warren county, was in attendance. OWEN DAVIS, the owner of the mill, who, by the way, was a brave Indian fighter, as well as a kind-hearted, obliging man, charged this Warren county man with speculating in pork, alias stealing his neighbor's hogs. The insult was resented—a combat took place forthwith, in which DAVIS proved victorious. He then went into court, and planting himself in front of the judges, he observed, addressing himself particularly to one of them, "Well, Ben, I've whipped that d—d hog-thief—what's the damage—what's to pay? and thereupon, suiting the action to the word, he drew out his buckskin purse, containing eight or ten dollars, and slammed it down on the table—then, shaking his fist at the judge, whom he addressed, he continued, "Yes, Ben, and if you'd steal a hog, d—n you, I'd whip you too." He had, doubtless come to the conclusion, that, as there was a court, the luxury of fighting could not be indulged in gratis, and he was for paying up as he went. Seventeen witnesses were sworn and sent before the grand jury, and nine bills of indictment were found the same day—all for affrays and assaults and batteries committed after the court was organized. To these indictments the persons all pleaded guilty, and were fined—DAVIS among the rest, who was fined eight dollars for his share in the transactions of the day.

"The following is the first entry made on the record after the grand jury retired: 'The court then proceeded to examine the several candidates for the surveyor's office, and JAMES GALLOWAY, jun., being well qualified, was appointed surveyor for the said county.' On the second day of the term, JOSEPH C. VANCE, (father of ex-Governor VANCE, of Champaign county,) was appointed to make the necessary arrangements for establishing the seat of justice, who, with DAVID HUSTON and JOSEPH WILLSON, his securities, entered into a bond, with a penalty of fifteen hundred dollars, for the faithful performance of his duties. He surveyed and laid out the town of Xenia (which, by the way, is an old French word, signifying a new year's gift,) the same season, for at the next December term, he was allowed '$49.25 for laying off the town of Xenia, finding chainmen, making plats, and selling lots.' On the third day of the term, DANIEL SYMMES was allowed twenty dollars for prosecuting in behalf of the State. The presiding judge then left the court, but it was continued by the associate judges for the transaction of county business. In addition to the duties now pertaining to associate judges, they discharged the duties now performed by the board of county commissioners. ARCHIBALD LOWRY and GRIFFITH FOOS were each licensed to keep a tavern in the town of Springfield, on the payment of eight dollars for each license. A license was also granted to PETER BORDERS, to keep a tavern at his house, on the payment of four dollars, 'together with all legal fees.' So our old log-house has the honor of having the first learned court held within its rough walls; and, in addition to that, it was, in fact, the first *hotel* ever licensed in the county in which hog and hommony, and new corn whisky could be had in abundance. Perhaps the court was a little interested in granting the license. Like old Jack Falstaff, they might like 'to take their ease in their own inn.' JAMES GALLOWAY, sen., was appointed county treasurer. The court then adjourned, having been in session three days."

We here leave our road to Cleveland, for a moment, to notice the route from Xenia to Springfield, on the Sandusky route.

Xenia Station House—64 miles from Cincinnati. This is one of the best and most convenient stations on the line from Cincinnati to Cleveland. The Evening Express from Cleveland takes supper here, and it is said, there is no Railway station where travellers find things so comfortable and pleasant. Mr. Stark, the provider of the Station Hotel is one who spares no pains, and whose establishment would make a model for most of the railway stations. The Station House is to the left, separating the two railway tracks; one of which (to the right) goes to Columbus and Cleveland, and the other (to the left) goes to Springfield and Sandusky. We are now 64 miles from Cincinnati, and by the railway, through Springfield, 152 miles from Sandusky, and, by Columbus, 190 miles from Cleveland. On the latter route, we pass through the seat of State Government, and, if the traveller chooses, he may stop a day, and visit some of the largest and best managed public institutions in America. The Little Miami Railroad Company own this line to Springfield, twenty miles distant. We shall take the left hand track to the latter point, and then return to Xenia, on our route to Columbus and Cleveland.

Old Town—3½ miles beyond Xenia, is the Old Chillicothe of the Shawanese. The term "Chillicothe," is the name of a Shawanese tribe. To this term they added "*o-ta-ny*," signifying town. There were five Chillicothes; one at Frankfort, Ross county, on Paint creek; one at Westfall, Pickaway county; one at "Old Town," where we now are; one at Piqua, Miami county, and one on the Maumee. It was this "Chillicothe," (Old Town,) to which Boone was carried—the Shawanese—and where he saw the warriors assemble for an attack on Boonesborough, which induced his escape. There are some old houses here, but, as a town, it has been nearly abandoned.

Boone's Escape.—Three miles the other side of Xenia, at a place now called "Old Town," was the "Old Chillicothe" of the Shawanee Indians. There, for a time, the celebrated Boone, when captured by the Indians, resided, and was adopted into one of the principal Indian families. In fact, he made himself so useful, and so popular, that the Indians indulged him in much liberty, and he was present at their councils, and acquainted with all their proceedings. At one of their councils at Old Chillicothe, he discovered they were about to attack Boonesborough, his own place, and he instantly resolved to escape. At about three miles below Xenia, in the valley of Glady, (where we are) he found himself early in the morning, with only an old Indian, and one or two women near. Making a pretence of hunting, he bade them good morning, and pursued a straight line to Boonesborough, which he reached in time to save. The following is BOONE's own account of it, taken from "TRUMBULL's Indian Wars:"

"On the 10th of April, 1778, the Indians returned with me to Old Chillicothe, where we arrived on the 25th. This was a long and fatiguing march, although through an exceedingly fertile country, remarkable for springs and streams of water. At Chillicothe, I spent my time as comfortably as I could expect; was adopted according to their customs into a family, where I became a son, and had great share in the affections of my new parents, brothers, sisters, and friends. I was exceedingly familiar and friendly with them, always appearing as cheerful and contented as possible, and they put great confidence in me. I often went a hunting with them, and frequently gained their applause for my activity at our shooting-matches. I was careful not to exceed many of them in shooting, for no people are more envious than they in this sport. I could observe in their countenances and gestures the greatest expressions of joy when they exceeded me, and when the reverse happened, of envy. The Shawanese king took great notice of me, and treated me with profound respect and entire friendship, often entrusting me to hunt at my liberty. I frequently returned with the spoils of the woods, and as often presented some of what I had taken to him, expressive of duty to my sovereign. My food and lodging was in common with them; not so good, indeed, as I could desire, but necessity made every thing acceptable.

"I now began to meditate an escape, and carefully avoided giving suspicion. I continued at Chillicothe until the first day of June, when I was taken to the salt springs east of the Scioto, and there employed ten days in the manufacturing of salt. During this time I hunted with my Indian masters, and found the land, for a great extent about this river to exceed the soil of Kentucky.

"On my return to Chillicothe, one hundred and fifty of the choicest Indian warriors were ready to march against Boonesborough. They were painted and armed in a frightful manner. This alarmed me, and I determined to escape.

"On the 18th of June, before sunrise, I went off secretly, and reached Boonesborough, on the 20th, a journey of one hundred and sixty miles, during which I had only one meal. I found our fortress in a bad state, but we immediately repaired our flanks, gates, and posterns, and formed double bastions, which we completed in ten days. One of my fellow prisoners escaped, after me, and brought advice that, on account of my flight, the Indians had put off their expedition for three weeks."

BOWMAN'S BATTLE.—Near this spot a Battle took place between the Indians and whites, under Col. BOWMAN, from Boonesborough. The following account of it is from "BOONE'S Narrative."

"In July, 1779, during my absence, Col. BOWMAN, with one hundred and sixty men, went against the Shawanese of Old Chillicothe. He arrived undiscovered. A battle ensued, which lasted until ten in the morning, when Col. BOWMAN retreated thirty miles. The Indians collected all their strength and pursued him, when another engagement ensued for two hours, not to Col. BOWMAN'S advantage. Col. HARROD proposed to mount a number of horses and break the enemy's line, who at this time fought with remarkable fury. This desperate measure had a happy effect, and the savages fled on all sides. In these two engagements we had nine men killed and one wounded. Enemy's loss uncertain. Only two scalps were taken."

YELLOW SPRINGS.—This is a celebrated place, one of the most beautiful to be anywhere found. Neither the Spring nor the surrounding grounds can be seen from the Station. There is a thriving little village round the Station House; but the "Springs" proper are to the right, over a creek, which flows amid rugged rocks. Just beyond is a plain, on which the native trees still stand. In the midst is a lawn, green and shady, with numerous cedars and evergreens. On one side of this is a long range of wooden buildings, which were formerly occupied as boarding houses, but are now only occupied by a private family. Near this again is the "Yellow Spring." This is a very large and extraordinary fountain of Chalybeate water, holding in solution a sort of red ochre, which tinges the water with a sort of orange or yellow color. It deposits a great deal of ochre, as it

flows out over the ground, and formerly a person employed himself here, in making large quantities of paint from this orange earth. This fountain is said to pour forth 110 gallons per minute! They flow off into the rocky creek below, in whose valley and banks are numerous wild and beautiful walks. The waters are chalybeate, and therefore tonic; but it is the excitement of the Highland air, the novelty of evergreens, in this rich country, the free exercise induced by the beautiful scenery which call up lively though lovely sensations, and renew with health the cheek of the invalid. I remember, many years since, to have arrived at Yellow Springs, convalescent from the billious fever. After a night's rest, and a tumbler of the fresh chalybeate, I ate a breakfast, fit for a wagoner, and taking a rifle, was decoyed, by a flock of wild ducks, from place to place, up this creek, till the day was declining, and then ate such a supper, with such an appetite, as only a famished soldier can be supposed to equal. The invalid disappeared, and I grew rugged and stalwart, buoyant and happy, amidst these beautiful scenes, and this health-beaming air.

Tawawa.—Xenia Springs.—We give a view of the Xenia Springs at a place called Tawawa, about two miles from Xenia

Station, as pleasant a place to sojourn at as can any where be found. There are a large number of acres of ground, all of which is forest belonging to the Springs.

This popular watering-place has undergone a change in the administration by the formation of a Joint Stock Association, which we hope and predict will redound greatly to the credit of its enterprising and persevering projectors and proprietors, and also to the future advantage of the health-seeking and pleasure-loving public. Enterprises of such pith and importance to the public should *belong to the public*, and we much mistake the craving need for ten years, and the present want of just such an accessible, delightful resort, as these Springs are to Ohio, if this enterprise be not eminently successful, and the stock as valuable as any of the kind.

The entire property is now held in trust by the Hon. Judge McLean, Hon. Judge Wright, Robert Buchanan, Thomas T. Whitehead, and Wm. Aug. Goodman, Esqs., of Cincinnati. The stock is divided into one thousand shares, of one hundred dollars each, and at the price (cost) at which the proprietors propose to dispose of a part of it, not only cannot fail to pay a very handsome dividend, but will be a good speculation, as there are many reasons why it will be a ten per cent. stock, *at*, or even *above* par. The improvements are upon the handsomest and most extensive scale. Their Dining-room seats seven hundred and thirty persons. Their Parlor is about forty feet square. The building itself is one hundred and fifty feet front, running back two hundred feet, part of which is four stories high, and contains about one hundred and fifty rooms, airy, high and light, and the whole establishment elegantly furnished in the most approved modern style. Their culinary and laundry operations are carried on by steam, and are said to be the most complete in the West. The conveniences for warm, cold, shower, vapor, and medicated Baths, surpass any Hotel attachments.

We may say, in regard to this watering place, in brief, further:

The house is situated in a beautiful grove of natural forest trees, surrounding the place on every side, affording a grateful shade.

The grounds are beautifully, tastefully, and extensively laid off, in walks and plats, within the shade, to and from the

VIEW OF TAWAWA SPRINGS.

Springs, and affording walks of several miles in extent. The ground is sandy and rolling, so that it is always dry and healthful.

In front of the house is a lawn of several acres of ground, tastefully laid out, and beautified with a fountain, and the ground shaded with native trees and shrubbery. The whole surrounded with beautiful cottages, forming one of the best play grounds for children, and shaded breathing spot for ladies and the feeble.

There are many delightful and romantic rides in many directions, over good roads.

There are scenes of romantic interest made memorable by Indian incident.

There are several distinct varieties of mineral waters. A chalybeate spring, which was known formerly by an Indian title, signifying, "Bath of Gold," in the Shawanese tongue, (termed so from the bright metallic color given to the stones over which the water flows.) This spring runs about eighteen gallons per minute, and is remarkably free from lime or sulphur, but is strongly impregnated with carbonate of iron. It rises in a basin of its own, on a side hill, and has, in time, worn a passage for itself, to the deep valley beneath, over shelving banks, known among the old settlers for fifty years, as the "Shawanee Baths;" having been used for bathing by that tribe of Indians. And, as late as 1800, the remains of the hollowed logs to conduct the water, and arrangements for shower-bathing were still extant.

There is a spring of white sulphur water and twenty or thirty other springs, some mineral, some pure water.

At one of the springs, there is a small lake and fountain.

There is a Gymnasium and Calisthenic department.

There are two Bowling Saloons, Billiard Tables, Shooting Gallery, Bathing department, &c.

The springs are within a mile of the Railroad and two miles from Xenia, on the Columbus McAdam Turnpike.

Passengers by the Railroad stop at Xenia, where an omnibus is ready, on arrival of the cars, to convey them to the Springs. The omnibus runs in connection with the trains.

Travellers desiring to rest part of a day, or over night, can leave their baggage safely at the Xenia Station, and will find this as pleasant a stopping place as at Columbus. It is especially convenient to passengers from Cincinnati East, who dedesire to avoid leaving early in the morning. By taking the afternoon train from Cincinnati, passengers get to the Springs some hours before dark, and leave next morning at 9 o'clock.

CLIFTON, OR FALLS OF THE MIAMI are four miles to the right, and away from the road. Before the manufacturing town, called Clifton, was built here, this was one of the resorts of the Springs visitors. The Little Miami was there compressed within a very narrow channel, running between lofty ledges of solid rock, till at length it leaps over a fall, and descends to a placid stream, coursing through level fields. The water has since been used for power, and the town of Clifton built on the side. The transmutation of what was once the wild and romantic Falls of the Miami, into a manufacturing village, reminds one of what was once said by a plain farmer, on visiting the Falls of Niagara. "Well, what do you think of it?" said his friend. "Think? It is a glorious place *for washing sheep!*" So is all beauty, and all romance dwindled away before the utilities of common life. *Cui bono?* is the question.

We now return to the Columbus Railroad, the first station of which is

CEDARVILLE—72½ miles from Cincinnati, and 46 from Columbus. The village is to the left, almost hid by the trees. Cedarville is on Massie's creek, a branch of the Little Miami, and is so called, from the cedar which grew abundantly on the creek; but, which, the traveler will remark, is not to be seen between this place and Cincinnati. Formerly there was a wild and picturesque view to be seen on the banks of Massie's creek, near Cedarville, but time, the axe, and the settlements have nearly destroyed its original beauty.

There are many evidences that this creek was a favorite residence of the savages in early times. Hereabout the spies used to take the greatest caution, and at night never built a fire. In dead winter, when warmth was needed, they dug a hole, built a smothered fire, and sitting over it, gathered warmth from the ascending smoke and adjoining ground. We give in the sketch below a view of one of the ancient remains which abounded—but few vestiges of this or most others remain. The line of embankment and of regular fortification can still be traced amid the fallen and decayed timber and the moss-covered earth, sufficient to show that a people of considerable cultivation at one period inhabited this valley of the West.

SOUTH CHARLESTON—82½ miles from Cincinnati, and 36 from Columbus. The Railway here passes into one corner of Clarke county, (Madison township,) of which South Charleston is a town. It is only a country village, but in one of the most beautiful districts in the entire Union. The lands have here the gentlest possible roll of the surface, as if the fields had been waves of the sea, gently subsiding when the winds went down. Most of the lands are pasture fields, on which are fed large flocks of sheep. The green meadows and the distant woods contrast well together.

The view we now give may be frequently seen between Xenia and Columbus, and, indeed, on most of the road west of them. On either side extensive grazing grounds, covered with cattle, or, with fields of grain.

The country from Xenia to Columbus is almost level, yet sufficiently rolling to carry off and thus prevent stagnant water. There are several creeks of considerable note, which cross the road and traverse the country, into which is emptied the small rivulets. The ground is filled with springs, and the country is rich and healthful. In the cut on next page is pictured what may be considered a continuous picture of the country. Extensive fields and rich crops are to be seen on either hand, and sometimes for a long distance the road is bounded by fields of grain.

Grazing may, however, be considered a distinct feature of this section of the State, and farms of a thousand acres are appropriated to this use. Some of the best cattle are purchased in this vicinity, and cattle trading is a separate business. Very large herds of cattle are at times seen in the fields adjoining the road. Many fortunes have already been made, and the business is still prosperous.

Madison County Line--89 miles from Cincinnati and 29 from Columbus. Madison county is one of some half dozen lying together, which exhibit a section of land, and natural scenery, unlike any other part of Ohio ; and unlike any of the States, except some in the extreme West. These counties are Fayette, Madison, Union, Crawford, Wyandot, and parts of Marion, Champaign, Logan, and Hardin. The surface of the country is nearly level, but drained by abundant and numerous streams, with slightly rolling plains. It is not entirely prairie, nor is it forest. It is in fact small prairies, interspersed with clumps of woods. Many parts of Madison county are like the English parks, or like the wood pastures round Lexington, (Ky.,) wanting only the neatness of cultivation. These lands were called "Barrens," by the settlers, because they wanted woods, and were supposed to be unproductive. But never was the term more misapplied. These lands are in fact, very rich, and are now becoming very valuable. The south side of this county is mostly occupied for pasturage and meadow; and used as grazing grounds for immense herds of cattle fattening for the eastern markets. The young cattle are bought principally in Illinois and Missouri, driven into Ohio, and here grazed, and fed on Indian corn till fattened for New York and Philadelphia. The adjoining county of Pickaway, where Indian corn is the chief staple, is estimated by the Agricultural Society to have exported 7,000 cattle in a year.

The following are the statistics of Madison county:

Surface....................	495 square miles.
Acres....................	282,000
Acres of Corn planted.......	19,278
Production of Corn........	610,930 bushels.
Average per acre..........	32 "
Acres of Wheat planted.....	4,019
Production of Wheat..,,...	64,610 bushels.
Average per acre..........	16 "
Number of Cattle.........	15,142
Number of Horses.........	4,324
Number of Sheep..........	51,818
Number of Swine..........	15,880
Assessed Value of property...	$3,662,665
Assessed Value to each Family of 6 persons............	2,200
Population..............	10,012

It will be remarked, that the amount of ploughed land is small, while, from the large number of cattle and sheep, we see there must be an extensive surface of pasture. It will also be seen, that the average wealth of each family is greater in this county, than in almost any other. The population is small, while the lands are valuable. There are many farms in this county, of from one to four thousand acres each; and some of them present a very pleasing rural scene—green fields of thousands of acres, interspersed with islands of trees, while herds of cattle are grazing around.

LONDON—94 miles from Cincinnati, and 24 from Columbus. Nobody will mistake this for the Metropolitan London; nor is there much prospect, they will ever be rivals. This is the county seat of Madison, and is a plain, unpretending country village. We stop at the station. The town is to the left, about a quarter of a mile. London contains about 600 inhabitants, three churches, a classical academy, and county buildings.

THE SPRINGFIELD AND LONDON RAILROAD will here intersect the Xenia and Columbus line. It is 19 miles in length, forming a connecting link between Columbus and Springfield. It will be 43 miles by Railroad from Columbus to Springfield, and 128 miles, by way of London, Springfield, and Dayton, to Cincinnati.

WEST JEFFERSON, 103 miles from Cincinnati, and 15 from Columbus, is a small town on the National Road, has 300 inhabitants, a church and several stores. In this grazing country, where farms are immensely large, and population sparse, the towns are all small. The traveler will notice, through all this region, there are no hills, no rocks, no abrupt eminences, and but few large forest trees. The land is level or gently rolling, and the woods are of a recent growth.

Darby Creek—crossed on a small frame bridge, is just beyond Jefferson, and, in pioneer annals, quite a celebrated stream. It rises in the north part of Madison county, and joins the Scioto near Circleville, Pickaway county. Many wild stories of Indian life are connected with Darby Creek. Among those which are true, and form a part of the history of the country, is that of the Capture, Life, and Return of Jonathan Alder, who lived near this, on Darby. We extract a part of it from Howe's History of Ohio, who took it from the manuscripts of Alder:

"Jonathan Alder was born in New Jersey, about eight miles from Philadelphia, September 17th, 1773. When at about the age of seven years, his parents removed to Wythe county, Virginia, and his father soon after died.

"In the succeeding March, (1782,) while out with his brother David, hunting for a mare and her colt, he was taken prisoner by a small party of Indians. His brother, on the first alarm, ran, and was pursued by some of the party. 'At length,' says Alder, 'I saw them returning, leading my brother, while one was holding the handle of a spear, that he had thrown at him and run into his body. As they approached, one of them stepped up and grasped him around the body, while another pulled out the spear. I observed some flesh on the end of it, which looked white, which I supposed came from his entrails. I moved to him, and inquired if he was hurt, and he replied that he was. These were the last words that passed between us. At that moment he turned pale and began to sink, and I was hurried on, and shortly after saw one of the barbarous wretches coming up with the scalp of my brother in his hand, shaking off the blood.'

"The Indians having also taken prisoner a Mrs. Martin, a neighbor to the Alders, with her young child, aged about four or five years, retreated towards their towns. Their route lay through the woods to the Big Sandy, down that stream to the Ohio, which they crossed, and thence went overland to the Scioto, near Chillicothe, and so on to a Mingo village on Mad river.

"Finding the child of Mrs. Martin burdensome, they soon killed and scalped it. The last member of her family was now destroyed, and she screamed in agony of grief. Upon this, one of the Indians caught her by her hair, and drawing the edge of his knife across her forehead, cried "sculp! sculp!" with the hope of stilling her cries. But, indifferent to life, she continued her screams, when they procured some switches and whipped her until she was silent. The next day, young ALDER having not risen, through fatigue, from eating, at the moment the word was given, saw, as his face was to the north, the shadow of a man's arm, with an uplifted tomahawk. He turned, and there stood an Indian, ready for the fatal blow. Upon this he let down his arm, and commenced feeling of his head. He afterwards told ALDER it had been his intention to have killed him; but, as he turned, he looked so smiling and pleasant, that he could not strike, and on feeling of his head and noticing that his hair was very black, the thought struck him, that if he could only get him to his tribe, he would make a good Indian; but that all that saved his life was the color of his hair.

"After they crossed the Ohio, they killed a bear, and remained four days to dry the meat for packing, and to fry out the oil, which last they put in the intestines, having first turned and cleaned them.

"The village to which ALDER was taken belonged to the Mingo tribe, and was on the north side of Mad river, which, we should judge, was somewhere within or near the limits of what is now Logan county. As he entered, he was obliged to run the gauntlet, formed by young children, armed with switches. He passed through this ordeal with little or no injury, and was adopted into an Indian family. His Indian mother thoroughly washed him with soap and warm water, with herbs in it, previous to dressing him in the Indian costume, consisting of a calico shirt, breech clout, leggins, and moccasons. The family, having thus converted him into an Indian, were much pleased with their new member. But JONATHAN was at first very homesick, thinking of his mother and brothers. Everything was strange about him; he was unable to speak a word of their language; their food disagreed with him; and, child-like, he used to go out daily for more than a month, and sit under a large walnut tree near the village, and cry for hours at a time over his deplorable situation. His Indian father was a chief of the Mingo tribe, named Succohanos; his Indian mother was named Whinecheoh, and their daughters respectively answered to the good old English names of Mary, Hannah, and Sally. Succohanos and Whinecheoh were old people, and had lost a son, in whose place they had adopted JONATHAN. They took pity on the little fellow, and did their best to comfort him, telling him that he would one day be restored to his mother and brothers. He says of them 'they could not have used their own son better, for which they shall always be held in most grateful remembrance by me.' His Indian sister Sally, however, treated him 'like a slave,' and, when out of humor, applied to him, in the Indian tongue, the unlady-like epithet of 'onorary, [mean,] lousy prisoner!' JONATHAN, for a time, lived with Mary, who had become the wife of the chief, Col. Lewis. 'In the fall of the year,' says he, 'the Indians would generally collect at our camp, evenings, to talk over their hunting expeditions. I would sit up to listen to their stories, and would frequently fall asleep just where I was sitting. After they left, Mary would fix my bed, and with Col. Lewis, would carefully take me up and carry me to it. On these occasions they would often say—supposing me to be asleep—'Poor fellow! we have sat up too long for him, and he has fallen asleep on the cold ground;' and then how softly would they lay me down and cover me up. Oh! never have I, nor can I, express the affection I had for these two persons.'

"JONATHAN, with other boys, went into Mad river to bathe, and on one occasion came near drowning. He was taken out senseless, and some time elapsed ere he recovered. He says, 'I remember, after I got over my strangle, I became very sleepy, and thought I could draw my breath as well as ever. Being overcome with drowsiness, I laid down to sleep, which was the last I remember. The act of drowning is nothing, but the coming to life is distressing. The boys, after they had brought me to, gave me a silver buckle, as an inducement not to tell the old folks of the occurrence, for fear they would not let me come with them again; and so the affair was kept secret.'

"When ALDER had learned to speak the Indian language, he became more contented. He says, 'I would have lived very happy, if I could have had health; but for three or four years I was subject to very severe attacks of fever and ague. Their diet went very hard with me for a long time. Their chief living was meat and hommony; but we rarely had bread, and very little salt, which was extremely scarce and dear, as well as milk and butter. Honey and sugar were plentiful, and used a great deal in their cooking, as well as on their food.'

"When he was old enough, he was given an old English musket, and told that he must go out and learn to hunt. So he used to follow along the water courses where mud turtles were plenty, and commenced his first essay upon them. He generally aimed under them, as they lay basking on the rocks; and when he struck the stone, they flew sometimes several feet in the air, which afforded great sport for the youthful marksman. Occasionally he killed a wild turkey, or a raccoon; and when he returned to the village with his game, generally received high praise for his skill—the Indians telling him he would make 'a great hunter one of these days.'

He was with the Indian squaws at the time of Crawford's defeat—was at the Mackacheah towns when destroyed by LOGAN, and remained with the Indians until after WAYNE'S Treaty, in 1795.

"When the settlers first made their appearance on Darby, ALDER could scarcely speak a word of English. He was then about twenty-four years of age, fifteen of which had been passed with the Indians. Two of the settlers kindly taught him to converse in English. He had taken up with a squaw for a wife, some time previous, and now began to farm like the whites. He kept hogs, cows, and horses, sold milk and butter to the Indians, horses and pork to the whites, and accumulated property. He soon was able to hire white laborers, and being dissatisfied with his squaw—a cross, peevish woman—wished to put her aside, get a wife from among the settlers, and live like them. Thoughts, too, of his mother and brothers began to obtrude, and the more he reflected, his desire strengthened to know if they were living, and to see them once more. He made inquiries for them, but was at a loss to know how to begin, being ignorant of the name of even the State in which they were. When talking one day with JOHN MOORE, a companion of his, the latter questioned him where he was from. ALDER replied, that he was taken prisoner somewhere near a place called Greenbriar, and that his people lived by a lead mine, to which he used to go frequently to see the hands dig ore. MOORE then asked him if he could recollect the names of any of his neighbors. After a little reflection, he replied, 'Yes, a family of Gulions that lived close by us.' Upon this, MOORE dropped his head as if lost in thought, and muttered to himself, 'Gulion! Gulion!' and then raising up, replied, 'My father and myself were out in that country, and we stopped at their house over one night, and if your people are living, I can find them.'

"Mr. MOORE, after this, went to Wythe county, and inquired for the family of ALDER; but without success, as they had removed from their former residence. He put up advertisements in various places, stating the facts, and where ALDER was to be found, and then returned. ALDER now abandoned all hopes of finding his family, supposing them to be dead. Some time after, he and MOORE were at Franklinton, when he was informed there was a letter for him in the post office. It was from his brother Paul, stating that one of the advertisements was put up within six miles of him, and that he got it the next day. It contained the joyful news that his mother and brothers were alive.

"ALDER, in making preparations to start for Virginia, agreed to separate from his Indian wife, divide the property equally, and take and leave her with her own people at Sandusky. But some difficulty occurred in satisfying her. He gave her all the cows, fourteen in number, worth $20 each, seven horses, and much other property, reserving to himself only two horses and the swine. Besides these, was a small box, about six inches long, four wide, and four deep, filled with silver, amounting probably to about $200, which he intended to take, to make an equal division. But to this she objected, saying the box was hers before marriage, and she would not only have it, but all it contained. ALDER says, 'I saw I could not get it without making a fuss, and probably having a fight, and told her that if she would promise never to trouble nor come back to me, she might have it; to which she agreed.'"

He then went to Virginia, and had the satisfaction of again seeing his mother and brothers.

"When I told my brother that my name was ALDER, he rose to shake hands with me, so overjoyed that he could scarcely utter a word, and my old mother ran, threw her arms around me, while tears rolled down her cheeks. The first words she spoke, after she grasped me in her arms, were 'How you have grown!' and then she told me of a dream she had. Says she, 'I dreamed that you had come to see me, and that you was a little *onorary* [mean] looking fellow, and I would not own you for my son; but now I find I was mistaken, and that it is entirely the reverse, and I am proud to own you for my son.' I told her I could remind her of a few circumstances that she would recollect, that took place before I was made captive. I then related various things, among which was that the negroes, on passing our house on Saturday evenings to spend Sundays with their wives, would beg pumpkins of her, and get her to roast them for them against their return on Monday morning. She recollected these circumstances, and said she had now no doubt of my being her son. We passed the balance of the day in agreeable conversation, and I related to them the history of my captivity, my fears and doubts, of my grief and misery the first year after I was taken. My brothers at this time were all married, and Mark and John had moved from there. They were sent for, and came to see me; but my half brother John had moved so far that I never got to see him at all."

FRANKLIN COUNTY LINE—14 miles from Columbus. Franklin county is one of the largest, and the most fertile in the State, and as it contains the seat of State government, is one with which is connected much of State and Local interest. The following are the statistics of the county:

Surface	529	square miles.
Number of acres	335,145	
Number of acres in Corn	51,842	
Production of Corn	1,984,929	bushels.
Average production per acre	39	"
Number of acres in Wheat	16,071	
Production of Wheat	294,162	bushels.
Average production of Wheat per acre	18	"
Number of Horses	9,848	
Number of Cattle	14,849	
Number of Sheep	26,811	
Number of Swine	35,722	
Assessed Value of Property	$11,981,221	
Population	42,880	
Assessed Value of Property to each Family of 6 Persons	$1,700	

It will be seen that an immense amount of corn is raised in this county, but that the average wealth is not so great as in Madison county, through which we have just passed. The reason is, that in a large town, like Columbus, there are great numbers of persons who own, comparatively nothing, and thus go to diminish the general average of property.

Franklin county is situated in the centre of the State, and is most admirably watered. The Scioto flows through its midst, and near Columbus is joined by the Olentangey or Whetstone river. On the west, Darby flows through the southern part, and on the east, the Big Walnut comes in from the South.

FRANKLINTON—one mile from Columbus, on the west bank of the Scioto. This town was laid out in 1797, was the seat of justice for the county till 1824, when Columbus became so. In the war of 1812-15, it was a place of considerable importance, being the rendezvous of the troops, sometimes amounting to several thousands. But, after Columbus became the seat of

State Government, and the war ended, Franklinton declined and Columbus rose.

Penitentiary Railroad.—To the left may be seen the track of another railway. This is merely for the use of the Penitentiary, in transporting stone from the quarries to be dressed by the convicts.

Scioto Bridge.—We now pass the Scioto river by a wooden bridge, and into the town of Columbus, with the Penitentiary in sight, an immense stone building on the left.

Scioto River.—This is one of the most important streams in the State. Rising near the west line of Hardin county, and interlocking with the branches of the Little and Great Miamis, it pursues a course of nearly 150 miles, till it joins the Ohio (at Portsmouth) 110 miles above Cincinnati. The Scioto Valley, so called, contains about 6,000 square miles of surface, and some of the richest lands in the State. From Columbus to Portsmouth is 90 miles, and at the middle point between them is Chillicothe, a town of 7,000 inhabitants, and surrounded by a rich and beautiful country.

Columbus—the Capital of Ohio, 118½ miles from Cincinnati, and 135 from Cleveland, is now before us. It happens here, as it does in nearly all towns and cities, that the Railway Station is just where nothing can be seen. The Railway station at Columbus is on the north side of the town, near the Penitentiary. Unless the traveller can find time to stop a few hours at Columbus, he will see little of one of the handsomest towns in the country. In the mean while, we will note some of its principal features for his use.

Columbus lies on the great plain of Central Ohio, on the east bank of the Scioto river. Not a mountain, not a hill, not a precipice, or rock is to be seen anywhere. The horizon seems to float away in the misty distance, or against the green woods, while all around spreads a rich, arable land, through which the Scioto winds its way. Looking to the west, the Scioto river is seen apparently much below the town, but really only a few feet; on its west shore, the broad bottoms, on which stands

Franklinton; and, beyond a slightly rising slope, just above Columbus, and in sight, the Scioto is joined by the Olentangey, or Whetstone river, its largest branch, flowing from the north.

Columbus was not laid out till 1812, and the Legislature commenced its sessions there in 1816. The rapidity of its improvement since may be known by the following table of its population at different times:

In 1820 population	········ 1,400		
In 1830 "	········ 2,437—	74 per cent.	increase.
In 1840 "	········ 6,048—	150 " "	"
In 1850 "	········17,100—	180 " "	"

It will be seen that not only the increment, but the *ratio* of increase in Columbus has been continually enlarging. When this is the case, it is not easy to make an estimate of future increase. We may, however, assume, with some confidence, that, in ten years more, it will have some 30 or 40,000 inhabitants, and take rank in the third class of American cities.

THE PUBLIC BUILDINGS of Columbus are remarkable, and some of them equal to any in the United States. Except the county Court House, a very beautiful building, they are all built by the State.

THE NEW CAPITOL OF OHIO.—At the present time, the Capitol is but one story high, and shows but little of the fine proportions which it will ultimately have. It is built of Ohio marble, a light grey limestone, which is at once durable and handsome. The new Capitol of Ohio is the largest building of the kind in in America, except one, the Capitol of the United States, at Washington. The following are the dimensions of some of the State Capitols:

The Capitol of Ohio, at Columbus, 304 by 184, covers an area of - - - - - - -	55,936	square feet.
The Capitol of Tennessee, at Nashville, 135 by 240, covers an area of - - - - -	32,400	do
The Capitol of North Carolina, at Raleigh, 166 by 90 feet, covers an area of - - -	14,940	do
The Capitol of Pennsylvania, at Harrisburgh, 180 by 80 feet, covers an area of - - -	14,400	do

The Capitol of Indiana, at Indianapolis, 80 by 180 feet, covers an area of - - - -	14,400	square feet.
The Capitol of Vermont, at Montpelier, 150 by 100 and by 72 ft, covers an area of about	12,200	do
The Capitol of Massachusetts, at Boston, 173 by 61 feet, covers an area of - - - -	10,553	do
The Capitol of New York, at Albany, 115 by 90 feet, covers an area of - - - -	10,350	do
The Capitol of Virginia, at Richmond, covers an area of about - - - - - - - - -	10,300	do
The Capitol of South Carolina, at Columbia, 60 by 170 feet, covers an area of - - -	10,200	do
The Capitol of New Hampshire, at Concord, 126 by 49 feet, covers an area of - - -	6,174	do
The Capitol of New Jersey, at Trenton, 100 by 60 feet, covers an area of - - - -	6,000	do
The Capitol of Michigan, 90 by 60 feet, covers an area of - - - - - - - - -	5,400	do
The Capitol of Kentucky, at Frankfort, 86 by 54 feet, covers an area of - - - -	4,644	do

The following are the comparative dimensions of this building and the Capitol of the United States at Washington:

		Washington.		Columbus.
Ground covered, - - - -		61,693 square feet.		55,936
Senate, - - - - - - - -		2,980 " "		3,880
House within columns,	4,548	4,548	4,722	4,722
Semi-circular Lobby,	1,065		850	
Back of Speaker, -	1,064		——	5,572
	——	6,677		
Library, - - - - -	3,140			
Library of Senate, -	1,085			
	——	4,225		4,650
Rotunda—				
Diameter, - - - - - - -		90 feet.		64
Height, - - - - - - - -		120 "		157
From floor to eye of Dome,		96 "		124

This shows that the Capitol at Washington covers about one-tenth more ground than the New State House of Ohio. Comparing the two Houses of Representatives, it will be seen that the space within the columns, available for the seats of members, is greater in our building than at Washington; our Senate, also, has a very much larger room, and the floor of our Library is of greater area than both the Libraries at Washington. This parallel will fully satisfy any one that there is no part of our new building that will not furnish ample accommodation, both for the present and future wants of the State. An inspection of the work already done, will show that we are about to meet these wants with a building of the most permanent character, and the perspective view will show, that we desire to make an ornamental building without overstepping the bounds of republican simplicity.

THE PENITENTIARY stands near the Railway Station, as above. It is a very large and stately building—built of Ohio marble. The entire structure, workshops, and yards cover six acres of ground. Each wing contains 350 cells for prisoners—the cells being built of solid stone, with iron doors, and ranged in five tiers. The prisoners are mostly employed in useful manufactures, so that they yield the State a surplus above their expenses.

THE OHIO LUNATIC ASYLUM is one of the finest buildings of the kind anywhere to be found. It makes an immense hollow square. The center building is 296 feet in front, and 46 feet deep. The wings are 40 feet in front each, running back 218

feet, and projecting 11 feet from the center. The whole front is 376 feet, and the wings 218 feet each—making in fact, 418 feet on three fronts. This Institution has been very well managed, as the results show, in the cure of patients.

The following are the statistical results of thirteen years' experience, in the Ohio Lunatic Asylum, as reported to the Legislature, by Dr. S. Hanbury Smith.

Number Admitted	1841
" Cured	897
" Improved	137
" Stationary	263
" Died	241
Average Number in the Asylum	323
Per Cent. of Recoveries on all Cases	48 per ct.
" " " " Recent Cases	75 "
" " " " Old Cases	23 "

The chances of recovery for a lunatic are *four times as great*, when the patient is taken immediately to the Asylum, as when the case is suffered to become chronic.

Even this Asylum, large as it is, is by no means large enough for the State. The Legislature has, with commendable liberality, authorized the erection of two other Asylums in other parts of the State.

Ohio Asylum for the Deaf and Dumb.—This also is a large Institution, with about 130 pupils, who are well taught and provided for.

The Ohio Institution for the Education of the Blind has about 100 pupils, and is, in all respects, most interesting. It is entirely successful in educating, by raised letters, known by the touch, even those who have been born blind.

Columbus Station.—Usually the cars arrive here at 12 meridian, having made 118 miles in 5½ hours. When they arrive at noon or evening, most excellent refreshments may be obtained at the Station.

There is the whistle, and away we go again! We have 135 miles to go, and we must make it in less than six hours. The Railway from Columbus to Cleveland passes through a comparatively new country, and, in consequence of seeking the

lowest and most level ground, it actually avoids the oldest and most flourishing towns. Those it does pass, are some distance from the road, and sometimes not even in sight. The new towns are yet in their infancy, and have the scattered and ragged appearance which attends new settlements.

The country between Columbus and Cleveland was almost in an original wild state when the road was opened through it.

The country was level—the line of road, as far as the eye can reach, straight—the forest wild and grand; the dead timber, however, causing water to lie on the ground, and thus mar the scene. The cut represents a view which may be seen a thousand times between the points above. But we mark the state of it by the cut, that we may have a *record* to refer to a few years hence, when the forest will be cut down, the ground cleared, and the fields exhibit prosperous husbandry and an enterprising people. Already the steam saw mill is at work in a hundred places, and

even the horse-saw, as in the cut, will be seen at work on every hand. The timber is valuable, and is rapidly being carried off to a market. Steam saw mills will make rapid havoc with the timber, and the value of the land will cause owners to exert themselves to bring it to a productive state. At the station below, we see nought but forest—forest.

WORTHINGTON, 11 miles from Columbus and 124 from Cleveland, is in sight, about half a mile to the left. It was named from THOMAS WORTHINGTON, Governor, Senator, and Canal Commissioner, one of the most useful and distinguished men the State has ever had. It is in the township of Sharon, and was purchased entire by Col. KILBOURNE, as agent for an association formed in Granby, Connecticut. It was settled by one hundred settlers from Hartford, Connecticut, and Hampshire co., Massachusetts. The first cabin erected was used for a school-house and a church. It is a flourishing village of about 500 inhabitants.

OLD WATER STATION—14 miles from Columbus.

BERLIN—20 miles from Columbus.

DELAWARE COUNTY.—We have been a long while traversing Franklin county—some 35 miles altogether. We came in from the west, and have been going directly north. From Columbus we have gone up the Olentangey, and are now in the county of Delaware. This county lies on the Scioto, the Olentangey, and their branches—being thus well watered. It is either level or gently rolling land, and much of it of very good quality. The following brief statistics will give a better idea of it than a mere description in words can:

Surface······················	440 square miles.
Number of acres··············	283,385
Assessed Value of Property····	$4,241,145
Population ··················	21,814
Assessed Value of Property to each Family of six persons·······	$ 2,000
Number of Horses············	7,134
" of Cattle ············	13,570
" of Sheep·············	51,007
" of Swine············	18,192

Taken as a whole, Delaware is a very good county, though less cultivated than many others.

The view of Delaware in the cut is taken from the new track or cross road, which brings us not into, but to this suburb and in plain view of the chief town. From the road, as in the cut, are seen many of the principal buildings of the town.

This cut is at the branch or turn out road, passing near to Delaware.

Delaware is not on the main road, but is reached by a branch of 2 miles, which the regular train usually takes. It is 25 miles from Columbus, and the county seat of Delaware county.

Delaware is on the Olentangey river, and was laid out in 1806, by Col. Moses Byxbe and Henry Baldwin, of Pittsburgh. The first cabin was put up in 1807. The town was incorporated and the court house built in 1815. Delaware is a handsome and flourishing town. In 1850, it had 2,075 inhabitants—

one of the largest hotels in Ohio—two newspapers—a bank—six churches, and many mercantile establishments.

THE OHIO WESLEYAN UNIVERSITY is located at Delaware. It has a handsome endowment, and is in a prosperous condition, with from 150 to 200 students.

The following reminiscences may be interesting:

"EARLY CUSTOMS.—I learn from the old pioneers, that during the early period of the county, the people were in a condition of complete social equality; no aristocratic distinctions were thought of in society, and the first line of demarkation drawn was to separate the very bad from the general mass. Their parties were for raisings and log-rollings, and the labor being finished, their sports usually were shooting and gymnastic exercises with the men, and convivial amusements among the women; no punctilious formality, nor ignoble aping the fashions of licentious Paris, marred their assemblies, but all were happy, and enjoyed themselves in seeing others so. The rich and the poor dressed alike; the men generally wearing hunting shirts and buckskin pants, and the women attired in coarse fabrics produced by their own hands; such was their common and holiday dress; and if a fair damsel wished a superb dress for her bridal day, her highest aspiration was to obtain a common American cotton check. The latter, which now sells for a shilling a a yard, then cost one dollar, and five yards deemed an ample pattern; silks, satins, and fancy goods, that now inflate our vanity and deplete our purses, were not then even dreamed of. The cabins were furnished in the same style of simplicity; the bedstead was home-made, and often consisted of forked sticks driven into the ground with cross-poles to support the clap-boards or the cord. One pot, kettle, and frying-pan were the only articles considered indispensable, though some included the tea-kettle; a few plates and dishes upon a shelf in one corner, was as satisfactory as is now a cupboard full of china, and their food relished well from a puncheon table. Some of the wealthiest families had a few split-bottom chairs, but as a general thing, stools and benches answered the place of lounges and sofas, and at first the green sward or smoothly leveled earth served the double purpose of floor and carpet. Whisky toddy was considered luxury enough for any party—the woods furnished abundance of venison, and corn pone supplied the place of every variety of pastry. Flour could not for some time be obtained nearer than Chillicothe or Zanesville; goods were very high, and none but the most common kinds were brought here, and had to be packed on horses or mules from Detroit, or wagoned from Philadelphia to Pittsburgh, thence down the Ohio river in flat boats to the mouth of the Scioto, and then packed, or hauled up. The freight was enormous, costing often $4.00 per cwt. Tea retailed at from two to three dollars a pound, coffee 75 cents, salt $5 to $6 per bushel, (50 lbs.) The coarsest calicos were $1 per yard, whisky from $1 to $2 per gallon, and as much of the latter was sold as of all other articles, for several years after Delaware was laid out; but it must be remembered that this then was the border town, and had considerable trade with the Indians. It was the common practice to set a bottle on each end of the counter for customers to help themselves gratuitously to enable them to purchase advantageously! Many people suffered hardships and endured privations that now would seem unsupportable. In the fall of 1803, Henry Perry, after getting up his cabin near Delhi, left his two sons and returned to Philadelphia for the remainder of his family, but finding his wife sick, and afterwards being sick himself, could not get back till the next June. These two little boys, Levi and Reuben, only eleven and nine years old, remained there alone, eight months, fifteen miles from any white family, and surrounded by Indians, with no food but the rabbits they could catch in hollow logs; the remains of one deer that the wolves killed near them, and a little corn meal that they occasionally obtained of THOMAS CELLAR, by following down the "Indian trace." The winter was a severe one, and their cabin was open, having neither daubing, fire-place, nor chimney; they had no gun, and were wholly unaccustomed to forest life, being fresh from Wales and yet these little fellows not only struggled through, but actually made a considerable clearing! JACOB FOUST, at an early day, when his wife was sick and could obtain nothing to eat that she relished, procured a bushel of wheat, and throwing it upon his shoulders, carried it to Zanesville to get it ground—a distance of more than 75 miles, by the tortuous path he had to traverse, and then, shouldering his flour, he retraced his steps home, fording the streams and camping out nights."

There are several deep cuts along this line, which open to the traveller a wide extent of country, and some pleasing views. We present one of these views in the cut subjoined, near Ashley, looking south.

CARDINGTON—38 miles from Columbus and 97 miles from Cleveland—is in the county of Morrow, which has recently been set off

from the counties of Delaware, Marion, Knox, and Richland. This is a new village, but, from the look of it, quite a smart place.

Morrow County.—This county, as we have said, is a new one. Nevertheless, it has acquired for itself a character on the tax list and the production roll; so we can present a statistical view of it, as we have done of others.

Surface	400	square miles.
Number of acres	256,000	
Acres in Corn	16,154	
Corn produced	583,318	bushels.
Average per acre	39	"
Acres in Wheat	19,389	
Wheat produced	364,334	bushels.
Average per acre	19	"
Assessed Value of property	$3,130,594	
Population	20,240	
Average Property to each Family of six persons	1,500	
Number of Horses	6,630	
" " Cattle	13,059	
" " Sheep	65,849	
" " Hogs	13,964	

It will be seen that the average wealth of Morrow county is not equal to that of some other counties; but, on the other hand, it is quite a newly settled country.

Gilead Station.—Gilead is the county seat of Morrow, and formerly belonged to Marion. It is a small town of some 500 inhabitants and two or three churches.

Crawford County.—After leaving Morrow, the Railway just touches on the edge of Crawford county, which here lies to the west. As we shall have no other opportunity of mentioning this county, we shall interest the traveller, for a moment, in the melancholy story of the man from whom it is named. This was Col. WILLIAM CRAWFORD, of Virginia, who having taken the command of an expedition against the Indians, in 1782, was disastrously defeated, and himself burned at the stake. His execution took place near Tymochte, on the Sandusky river, on the limits of Wyandot, then Crawford county.

The annexed history of CRAWFORD's campaign we take from DODDRIDGE's Notes:

"CRAWFORD's campaign, in one point of view, at least, is to be considered as a second Moravian campaign, as one of its objects was that of finishing the work of murder and plunder with the Christian Indians at their new establishment on the Sandusky. The next object was that of destroying the Wyandot towns on the same river. It was the resolution of all those concerned in this expedition not to spare the life of any Indians that might fall into their hands, whether friends or foes. It will be seen in the sequel that the result of this campaign was widely different from that of the Moravian campaign the preceding March.

"It should seem that the long continuance of the Indian war had debased a considerable portion of our population to the savage state of our nature. Having lost so many relatives by the Indians, and witnessed their horrid murders and other depredations on so extensive a scale, they became subjects of that indiscriminating thirst for revenge which is such a prominent feature in the savage character, and having had a taste of blood and plunder without risk or loss on their part, they resolved to go on and kill every Indian they could find, whether friend or foe.

"Preparations for this campaign commenced soon after the return of the Moravian campaign in the month of March, and as it was intended to make what was called at that time "a dash," that is an enterprise conducted with secrecy and dispatch, the men were all mounted on the best horses they could procure. They furnished themselves with all their outfits except some ammunition, which was furnished by the Lieutenant Colonel of Washington county, Pennsylvania.

"On the 25th of May, 1782, 480 men mustered at the old Mingo towns, on the western side of the Ohio river. They were all volunteers from the immediate neighborhood of the Ohio, with the exception of one company from Ten Mile, in Washington county. Here an election was held for the office of commander-in-chief for the expedition. The candidates were Col. WILLIAMSON and Col. CRAWFORD; the latter was the successful candidate. When notified of his appointment, it is said he accepted it with apparent reluctance.

"The army marched along "Williamson's trail," as it was then called, until they arrived at the upper Moravian town, in the fields belonging to which there was still plenty of corn on the stalks, with which their horses were plentifully fed during the night of their encampment there.

"Shortly after the army halted at this place, two Indians were discovered by three men, who had walked some distance out of the camp. Three shots were fired at one of them, but without hurting him. As soon as the news of the discovery of Indians had reached the camp, more than one-half of the men rushed out without command, and in the most tumultuous manner, to see what happened. From that time, Col. CRAWFORD felt a presentiment of the defeat which followed.

"The truth is, that notwithstanding the secresy and dispatch of the enterprise, the Indians were beforehand with our people. They saw the rendezvous on the Mingo bottom, knew their number and destination. They visited every encampment immediately on their leaving it, and saw from the writing on the trees and scraps of paper that 'no quarter was to be given to any Indian, whether man, woman, or child.'

"Nothing material happened during their march until the 6th of June, when their guides conducted them to the site of the Moravian villages, on one of the upper branches of the Sandusky river; but here, instead of meeting with Indians and plunder, they met with nothing but vestiges of desolation. The place was covered with high grass, and the remains of a few huts alone, announced that the place had been the residence of the people whom they intended to destroy, but who had moved off to Scioto some time before.

"In this dilemma what was to be done? The officers held a council, in which it was determined to march one day longer in the direction of Upper Sandusky, and if they should not reach the town in the course of the day, to make a retreat with all speed.

"The march was commenced the next morning through the plains of Sandusky, and continued until about two o'clock, when the advance guard was attacked and driven in by the Indians, who were discovered in large numbers in the high grass, with which the place was covered. The Indian army was at that moment about entering a piece of woods, almost entirely surrounded by plains; but in this they were disappointed by a rapid movement of our men. The battle then commenced by a heavy fire from both sides. From a partial possession of the woods which they had gained at the onset of the battle, the Indians were soon dislodged. They then attempted to gain a small skirt of wood on our right flank, but were prevented from doing so by the vigilance and bravery of Maj. Leet, who commanded the right wing of the army at that time. The firing was incessant and heavy until dark, when it ceased. Both armies lay on their arms during the night. Both adopted the policy of kindling large fires along the line of battle, and then retiring some distance in the rear of them, to prevent being surprised by a night attack. During the conflict of the afternoon, three of our men were killed and several wounded.

In the morning our army occupied the battle ground of the preceding day. The Indians made no attack during the day, until late in the evening, but were seen in large bodies traversing the plains in various directions. Some of them appeared to be employed in carrying off their dead and wounded.

In the morning of this day, a council of the officers was held, in which a retreat was resolved on, as the only means of saving the army. The Indians appeared to increase in number every hour. During the sitting of this council, Col. Williamson proposed taking one hundred and fifty volunteers, and marching directly to Upper Sandusky. This proposition the commander-in-chief prudently rejected, saying, 'I have no doubt that you would reach the town, but you would find nothing there but empty wigwams, and having taken off so many of our best men, you would leave me the rest to be destroyed by the host of Indians with which we are now surrounded, and on your return they would attack and destroy you. They care nothing about defending their towns; they are worth nothing. Their squaws, children and property have been removed from them long since.

Our lives and baggage are what they want, and if they can get us divided they will soon have them. We must stay together and do the best we can.'

"During this day preparations were made for a retreat by burying the dead, burning fires over their graves to prevent discovery, and preparing means for carrying off the wounded. The retreat was to commence in the course of the night. The Indians, however, became apprized of the intended retreat, and about sundown attacked the army with great force and fury, in every direction excepting that of Sandusky.

"When the line of march was formed by the commander-in-chief, and the retreat commenced, our guides prudently took the direction of Sandusky, which afforded the only opening in the Indian lines and the only chance of concealment. After marching about a mile in this direction, the army wheeled about to the left, and by a circuitous route gained the trail by which they came, before day. They continued their march the whole of the next day, with a trifling annoyance from the Indians, who fired a few distant shots at the rear guard, which slightly wounded two or three men. At night they built fires, took their suppers, secured the horses, and resigned themselves to repose, without placing a single sentinel or vidette for safety. In this careless situation, they might have been surprised and cut off by the Indians, who, however, gave them no disturbance during the night, nor afterwards during their retreat. The number of those composing the main body in the retreat was supposed to be about three hundred.

"Most unfortunately, when a retreat was resolved on, a difference of opinion prevailed concerning the best mode of effecting it. The greater number thought best to keep in a body and retreat as fast as possible, while a considerable number thought it safest to break off in small parties and make their way home in different directions, avoiding the route by which they came. Accordingly many attempted to do so, calculating that the whole body of the Indians would follow the main army; in this they were entirely mistaken. The Indians paid but little attention to the main body of the army, but pursued the small parties with such activity that but very few of those who composed them made their escape.

"The only successful party who were detached from the main army was that of about forty men, under the command of a Captain WILLIAMSON, who, pretty late in the night of the retreat, broke through the Indian lines under a severe fire, and with some loss, and overtook the main army on the morning of the second day of the retreat.

"For several days after the retreat of our army, the Indians were spread over the whole country, from Sandusky to the Muskingum, in pursuit of the straggling parties, most of whom were killed on the spot. They even pursued them almost to the banks of the Ohio. A man, of the name of Mills, was killed, two miles to the eastward of the site of St. Clairsville, in the direction of Wheeling, from that place. The number killed in this way must have been very great, the precise amount, however, was never fairly ascertained.

"At the commencement of the retreat, Col. CRAWFORD placed himself at the head of the army and continued there until they had gone about a quarter of a mile, when missing his son, JOHN CRAWFORD, his son-in-law, Major HARRISON, and his nephews, Major ROSE, and WILLIAM CRAWFORD, he halted and called for them as the line passed, but without finding them. After the army had passed him, he was unable to overtake it, owing to the weariness of his horse. Falling in company with Dr. KNIGHT and two others, they travelled all the night, first north and then to the east, to avoid the pursuit of the Indians. They directed their course during the night by the north star.

"On the next day, they fell in with Captain JOHN BIGGS and Lieut. ASHLEY, the latter of whom was severely wounded. There were two others in company with BIGGS and ASHLEY. They encamped together the succeeding night. On the next day, they were attacked by a party of Indians, who made Col. CRAWFORD and Dr. KNIGHT prisoners. The other four made their escape, but Captain BIGGS and Lieut. ASHLEY were killed the next day.

Col. CRAWFORD and Dr. KNIGHT were immediately taken to an Indian encampment at a short distance from the place where they were captured. Here they found nine fellow-prisoners and seventeen Indians. On the next day, they were marched to the old Wyandot town, and on the next morning, were paraded, to set off, as they were told, to go to the new town. But alas! a very different destination awaited these captives! Nine of the prisoners were marched off some distance before the Colonel and the Doctor, who were conducted by Pipe and Wingenund, two Delaware chiefs. Four of the prisoners were tomahawked and scalped on the way, at different places.

"Preparations had been made for the execution of Col. CRAWFORD, by setting a post about fifteen feet high in the ground, and making a large fire of hickory poles about six yards from it. About half a mile from the place of execution, the remaining five of the nine prisoners were tomahawked and scalped by a number of squaws and boys. Col. CRAWFORD's son and son-in-law were executed at the Shawanese town. * * *

"Dr. KNIGHT was doomed to be burned at a town about forty miles distant from Sandusky, and committed to the care of a young Indian to be taken there. The first day they travelled about twenty-five miles, and encamped for the night. In the morning, the gnats being very troublesome, the Doctor requested the Indian to untie him that he might help him to make a fire to keep them off. With this request the Indian complied. While the Indian was on his knees and elbows, blowing the fire, the Doctor caught up a piece of a tent-pole, which had been burned in two, about eighteen inches long, with which he struck the Indian on his head with all his might, so as to knock him forward into the fire. The stick, however, broke, so that the Indian, although severely hurt, was not killed, but immediately sprang up; on this, the Doctor caught up the Indian's gun to shoot him, but drew back the cock with so much violence that he broke the spring. The Indian ran off with an hideous yelling. Doctor KNIGHT then made the best of his way home, which he reached in twenty-one days, almost famished to death. The gun being of no use, after carrying it a day or two, he left it behind. On his journey he subsisted on roots, a few young birds and berries."

We here pass over one of the branches of Whetstone creek, one of the favorite resorts of the Indians in early days, and near the head of one of the principal streams from which the Scioto derives its water. The country along this line of the creek is rich, and the timber heavy and valuable.

Galion--56 miles from Columbus and 79 from Cleveland, is in Richland county, and at the intersection of the Bellefontaine and Indiana Railroad with the Cleveland and Columbus Railroad. The Bellefontaine and Indiana line will soon be completed. That road is 108 miles in length in Ohio, extending from Galion through Marion to Bellefontaine, and thence to the

Indiana line, at Union, where it is prolonged in another work, to Indianapolis. On the east, it is intended to join the Ohio and Pennsylvania Railroad, which also intersects the Cleveland line, three and a half miles from this point.

Richland County.—This was one of the largest and most populous counties in the State, till large slices were cut off to form Ashland and Morrow. It is yet, however, large and important. The county has no river, but several streams and creeks that give it sufficient irrigation. On the west side are the head streams of Sandusky River, and on the east, the head waters of Mohican, one of the principal branches of the Muskingum. The land is rolling and well adapted to wheat.

The statistics of Richland county are as follows, viz :

Surface	512	square miles.
Number of acres	327,680	
Acres cultivated in Corn	16,300	
Corn produced	563,320	bushels.
Acres cultivated in Wheat	41,219	
Wheat produced	795,213	bushels.
Average Corn to an acre	38	"
Average Wheat to an acre	19½	"
Assessed Value of Property for Taxation	$5,925,737	
Population	30,877	
Property to each family of six persons	$1,150	
Number of Horses	8,503	
Number of Cattle	17,742	
Number of Sheep	72,764	
Number of Swine	23,103	

Either this county is assessed too low, or it is by no means wealthy, and yet the elements above exhibited are those of great agricultural wealth. It will be seen, that the proportion of wheat, cattle, and sheep are very large. After making a full allowance of bread for all the inhabitants of the county, it is plain, the people can export no less than 600,000 bushels of wheat! In fact, this and the adjoining counties are among the best in the Union for wheat.

Shelby—68 miles from Columbus, and 67 from Cleveland, is about half way, and usually the train from Cleveland dines here. There is little appearance of a town here, but one may be seen in the distance. The Station Houses are large and convenient. The *position* is one of great importance; for here is the intersection of two of the greatest railroad lines in the State—the Cincinnati and Cleveland, and the Sandusky, Newark, and Zanesville Line. It is the distributing point for a great number of passengers: for example, travellers coming from the East, by way of Cleveland or Pittsburgh, may here go to Sandusky, and the North, to wit: to Cincinnati and the South-West, or, to Zanesville and the centre of Ohio. So in coming from either of those directions, they may again diverge in any direction.

The Sandusky Railway passes through Mansfield, Mount Vernon, Newark, Zanesville, and the very heart of the State, and here trains are waiting to take the traveller in any direction.

Salem—from Columbus, 75 miles, from Cleveland, 60 miles, is a mere stopping place.

"At an early day, there was a very eccentric character who frequently was in this region, well remembered by the early settlers. His name was Jonathan Chapman, but he was usually known as *Johnny Appleseed.* He was originally, it is supposed, from New England.

"He had imbibed a remarkable passion for the rearing and cultivation of apple trees from the seed. He first made his appearance in Western Pennsylvania, and from thence made his way into Ohio, keeping on the outskirts of the settlements, and following his favorite pursuit. He was accustomed to clear spots in the loamy lands on the banks of the streams, plant his seeds, enclose the ground, and then leave the place, until the trees had in a measure grown. When the settlers began to flock in and open their 'clearings,' Johnny was ready for them with his young trees, which he either gave away or sold for some trifle, as an old coat, or any article of which he could make use. Thus he proceeded for many years, until the whole country was in a measure settled and supplied with apple trees, deriving self-satisfaction amounting almost to delight, in the indulgence of his engrossing passion. About twenty years since, he removed to the far West, there to enact over again the same career of humble usefulness.

"His personal appearance was as singular as his character. He was a small 'chunked' man, quick and restless in his motions and conversation; his beard and hair were long and dark, and his eye black and sparkling. He lived the roughest life, and often slept in the woods. His clothing was mostly old, being generally given to him in exchange for apple trees. He went barefooted, and often travelled miles through the snow in that way. In doctrine he was a follower of Swedenborg, leading a moral, blameless life, likening himself to the primitive Christians, literally taking no thought for the morrow. Wherever he went he circulated Swedenborgian works, and if short of them, would tear a book in two and give each part to different persons. He was careful not to injure any animal, and thought hunting morally wrong. He was welcome every where among the settlers, and treated with great kindness even by the Indians. We give a few anecdotes illustrative of his character and eccentricities.

"On one cool autumnal night, while lying by his camp fire in the woods, he observed that the musquitoes flew in the blaze and were burnt. Johnny, who wore on his head a tin utensil, which answered both as a cap and a mush pot, filled it with water and quenched the fire, and afterwards remarked, 'God forbid that I should build a fire for my comfort, that should be the means of destroying any of his creatures.' At another time, he made his camp fire at the end of a hollow log in which he intended to pass the night, but finding it occupied by a bear and her cubs, he moved his fire to the other end, and slept on the snow in the open air, rather than disturb the bear. He was one morning in a prairie, and was bitten by a rattlesnake. Some time after, a friend inquired of him about the matter. He drew a long sigh and replied, 'Poor fellow! he only just touched me, when I, in an ungodly passion, put the heel of my scythe upon him and went home. Some time after, I went there for my scythe, and there lay the poor fellow dead.' He bought a coffee bag, made a hole in the bottom, through which he thrust his head and wore it as a cloak, saying it was as good as any thing. An itinerant preacher was holding forth on the public square in Mansfield, and exclaimed, 'where is the bare-footed Christian, travelling to heaven?' Johnny, who was lying on his back on some timber, taking the question in its literal sense, raised his bare feet in the air, and vociferated '*here he is!*'"

Huron County.—We are now in the county of Huron, one of the twelve counties which constitute the Western Reserve, or, as formerly called, "New Connecticut." It is a curious fact, that before the Constitution was formed, and indeed after, Connecticut claimed, by virtue of the charter from Charles the Second, the whole country from that State to the western ocean! The reason was, that in those days, they knew nothing about the boundaries of America, and the Charter of Charles bounded the State by the Western Ocean! This ran over Western New York as well as a part of Pennsylvania. The result was, that the lands of New Connecticut (then belonging to the National Government in the North Western Territory) were given to the State of Connecticut for relinquishing her territorial rights. Hence it was the "Reserve," and hence also New Connecticut. The Railway passes through three counties of the Reserve—Huron, Lorain, and Cuyahoga, but, as usual, avoids most of the towns and improvements. The soil of the Reserve is not so good as that in the lower part of the State; but it is a good grazing country, raising many cattle and sheep, and exporting great quantities of butter, cheese, and wool.

Huron county is the western of the Reserve, and has a considerable variety in its lands. It is well watered by Huron and Vermillion rivers and their branches. On the west, it is almost entirely level, but where we now cross it, is gently undulating.

The statistics of Huron are as follows:

Surface	500	square miles.
Number of acres	320,000	
Number of acres in Corn	22,806	
Number of acres in Wheat	21,882	
Production of Corn	878,143	bushels.
Production of Wheat	441,604	"
Average production of Corn per acre	40	"
Average production of Wheat per acre	20	"

Assessed Value of Property for Taxation	$5,565,697
Population	26,203
Average assessment to each family of six persons	$1,340
Number of Cattle	19,282
Number of Horses	7,306
Number of Sheep	82,741
Number of Swine	14,389

The amount of grain raised, for the population, is very great, and the cattle and sheep are numerous.

GREENWICH—from Columbus, 81 miles, and from Cleveland, 54 miles, is merely a stopping point.

NEW LONDON—47 miles from Cleveland, is also in Huron county.

ROCHESTER—41 miles from Cleveland, is in Lorain county; and is merely a country township.

LORAIN COUNTY lies on Lake Erie, west of Cleveland. It is watered by Black river and its tributaries, and is on the whole a prosperous section of country. Its statistics are below:

Surface	500	square miles.
Number of acres	320,000	
Acres cultivated in Corn	12,925	
Production of Corn	446,224	bushels.
Acres in Wheat	11,555	
Production of Wheat	206,301	"
Average Corn to an acre	35	"
Average Wheat to an acre	18	"
Assessed Value of Property	$4,449,019	
Average assessment to each family of six persons	$1,030	
Population	26,091	
Number of Horses	6,519	
Number of Cattle	23.132	
Number of Sheep	80,880	
Number of Swine	9,950	

Cattle and sheep are numerous, but, as a whole, this county is not by any means so wealthy, proportionally as those in the middle and southern parts of the State.

WELLINGTON—36 miles from Cleveland.

PENFIELD—33 miles from Cleveland.

LAGRANGE—29 miles from Cleveland.

These are all merely country townships, which are named in order in which they come.

GRAFTON—25 miles from Cleveland, is important, because, here is the intersection of the Interior Lake Road, from Maumee Bay through Norwalk, with the Cleveland Road, which will make an important connection between the Eastern and Western Lines.

EATON—22 miles from Cleveland.

COLUMBIA—18 miles from Cleveland.

These also are only country townships through which the Railway passes.

OLMSTEAD—Cuyahoga county—15 miles from Cleveland, is also an intersection of the Lake Shore Railroad, from Sandusky, through Elyria, to Cleveland, Erie Dunkirk, and Buffalo.

CUYAHOGA COUNTY.—We are now in the county of Cuyahoga, whose principal town is Cleveland; and which is the most important county in Northern Ohio. It takes its name from the "CUYAHOGA" River, which, although not navigable—yet no doubt gave the first impulse to Cleveland, by causing the termination of the Ohio canal there. The Indian word "Cuyahoga" is said to mean crooked, and the river of that name is sufficiently so to justify the epithet.

The county of Cuyahoga is gently undulating; the soil is not very rich, but is well watered in every part, and being on the coast of Lake Erie, gives it great commercial advantages. It has bog-iron, sand-stone quarries, grindstones, and various incidental resources, which, united to its commerce, has given Cuyahoga a pretty rapid development.

One of the first settlements in the western country was made in this county, by the French, who, in 1755, had a trading house near the Mingo towns on the Cuyahoga river, about five miles from its mouth. In 1786, the Moravian Missionaries made a settlement here, and the British held possession till 1790. The first permanent settlement was made at Cleveland, in 1796. Since then the growth of Cuyahoga has been as follows viz:

In 1810	1,495	inhabitants.	
" 1820	6,328	"	300 per cent.
" 1830	10,362	"	66 " "
" 1840	26,512	"	160 " "
" 1850	48,105	"	85 " "

It will be seen that the growth of Cuyahoga has been very rapid, and is not likely to be less. The year 1860 will probably find Cuyahoga with 90,000 inhabitants. Its statistics in 1850 are as follows:

Surface	432	square miles.
Number of acres	281,093	
" acres cultivated in Corn	12,018	
" " " Wheat	6,711	
Production of Corn,	396,922	bushels.
" of Wheat	97,966	"
Average production of Corn per acre	33	"
Average production of Wheat	16	"

Number of Horses	7,089
" " Cattle	18,922
" " Sheep	59,056
" " Swine	8,400
" " Pleasure Carriages . .	1,619
" " Pianos	233
" " Watches	2,136
Assessed value of Property	$11,071,029
Average value of Property to each family of six persons. . .	$1,380

The amount of plowed land is small; but a large part of the land is used as pasturage. The wealth of the county is inferior to that of the southern section of the State, which is caused chiefly by the difference in the *arable* amount of land. The inhabitants are industrious, thrifty, and moral.

Berea—12 miles from Cleveland, is a pleasant village, and from the stream near it are some fine views.

Rockport—seven miles from Cleveland, is only a way station.

The approach to Cleveland is down a ravine leading to the river and over the canal. The city of Cleveland is seen in the cut, chiefly located on the rising ground, or upper plain above the river and canal. On the bottom are a large number of manufactories of great value. The city extends over a large space of ground, and this can be reasonably well extended by the extent of surface; and the tops of the houses are seen over the edge of the bank as the scene comes into view to the right in going into the city. To the left, the Cuyahoga river finds its way into the Lake; and the steamers and shipping which crowd the wharves along the river, give indication of the commercial importance of the city; the facts as to which are presented elsewhere. The road crosses one of the main streets of the city, and passes along down the lake to the depot near the pier and Lake shore, where are the workshops and places of business of the Company. The second cut shows the depot as seen from the end of the pier and light house.

Cleveland—the Forest City—is now before us, at the mouth of the Cuyahoga, on the shore of beautiful Lake Erie, and is, perhaps, the handsomest town in America. A few years since, we stood near the grave of Uncas, in the elegant town of Norwich, Connecticut. As we had walked up Washington street, lined with its beautiful trees, and its splendid residences, we remarked to a gentleman near, that that was probably the handsomest town in the United States. "No," said he, "there is one other handsomer." "What one?" said we. "Cleveland, Ohio. I never go there in my business, but what I linger and dally, till I am hurried away to make up time." We are inclined to think his verdict right, though such lovely places as Norwich, New Haven, Canandaigua, &c., may well claim a rivalry with it. How it was called "Forest City," we know not, though a friend who sometimes figures in the newspapers over the signature of "Otsego," claimed to have so baptized it. Its best streets are lined with lofty trees, giving it the rural and pleasant air which reminds us of a city in the forest.

Cleveland was named from General Moses Cleveland, who laid it out in 1796. He was born in Canterbury, Connecticut; was bred a lawyer, and practised his profession in his native town; to which he returned, and where he died, leaving a large fortune.

The settlement of Cleveland was attended with the usual difficulties and hardships of a new country, and for many years, the inhabitants were much troubled with fever and ague. All these troubles, however, are now over, and the town is on the high road to become a large city. The growth of Cleveland, since its settlement, has been as follows, viz:

In 1796 - - - - - - - - - - - -	3	inhabitants.
In 1798 - - - - - - - - - - - -	16	"
In 1825 - - - - - - - - - - - -	500	"
In 1831 - - - - - - - - - - - -	1,100	"
In 1835 - - - - - - - - - - - -	5,080	"
In 1840 - - - - - - - - - - - -	6,071	"
In 1846 - - - - - - - - - - - -	10,135	"
In 1850 - - - - - - - - - - - -	17,041	"

In 1840, the three towns of Cleveland, Columbus, and Dayton were almost exactly equal, each having, in round numbers, 6,000 inhabitants. In 1850, Columbus nominally had about 500 more than Cleveland, and both about 5,000 more than Dayton. But in fact, Cleveland was much the largest; for Ohio City, on the other side of the Cuyahoga, was not included. The true population of Cleveland was as follows, viz:

Cleveland, in the Corporation, - - - - - - -	17,041
Ohio City, - - - - - - - - - - - - - - -	6,375
East Cleveland, - - - - - - - - - - - - -	2,341
Total, - - -	25,757

This includes, of course, all the suburbs, and makes Cleveland, in magnitude, the *twenty-fourth* city of the United States.

The town is chiefly built on the upper level or high bank of the Lake, with very broad streets. It is dry and healthy, with fine views of the lake, the river, and the numerous water craft of the port. Near the center is a Public Square of ten acres, divided by intersecting streets. Its principal characteristics are:

1. Its Public Works. These are numerous and important.

The Ohio Canal terminates here, after traversing the entire State, from Portsmouth, on the Ohio River, a distance of about 320 miles. The business of this canal is immense, especially in grain, and gave the first impulse to Cleveland.

The PENNSYLVANIA AND OHIO CANAL, which comes from Beaver creek, below Pittsburgh, joins the Ohio Canal at Akron, Summit county, and thus also terminates, really, at Cleveland.

The CINCINNATI, COLUMBUS AND CLEVELAND RAILROAD, on which we have just been traveling, is another work, which has greatly benefitted Cleveland. It is 254 miles by Railroad from Cincinnati, and, as we have seen, one well managed, and pleasant to travel on, and passing through a rich country.

The CLEVELAND AND WELLSVILLE RAILROAD connects Cleveland with the Ohio river, directly south of it, by a line of something more than ninety miles in length.

The CLEVELAND AND PITTSBURGH RAILROAD connects Cleveland with Pittsburgh, by about 120 miles, of which 50 miles is a common track with the Wellsville Railroad.

THE LAKE SHORE RAILROAD extends from Toledo through Sandusky, Elyria, Cleveland, Painesville, Conneaut, &c., to Buffalo. This work is nearly completed, and a portion of it is in operation.

2. COMMERCE OF CLEVELAND.—As might be supposed, the commerce of Cleveland is very great. In the United States Steam Marine Report, made by the Secretary of the Treasury, the following is given as the statistics of steamers there:

Number of Steamers,	13
Tonnage of do	6,417
Crews,	217

There were built in 1850, two schooners and seven slooops, and the total amount of tonnage of sail vessels, was 25,321 tons. From the port of Cleveland there were cleared 238 vessels, carrying 31,929 tons.

The Report of the Board of public works in Ohio shows that the following amount of Domestic Produce was received at the Port of Cleveland, in 1851:

Flour	645,730 barrels.
Wheat	2,529,699 bushels.
Pork	12,011 barrels.
Whisky	44,843 "
Corn	998,059 bushels.
Bacon, in bulk	1,488,333 lbs.
Lard	1,281,368 "
Butter	1,164,185 "
Cheese	298,342 "
Tallow	248,546 "
Wool	2,172,829 "
Coal	2,992,343 bushels.

Seven bushels of wheat are considered a most ample allowance of bread for each individual. By that standard, there was bread enough shipped from Cleveland, in the form of flour, wheat, and corn, to feed a million of people! The total value of domestic produce shipped from Cleveland, and received from the Canal, must have exceeded seven millions of dollars! The commerce of Cleveland is likely to increase, as railroads shall concentrate there.

CHURCHES AND PUBLIC INSTITUTIONS.—There are in Cleveland about 25 churches, of almost every denomination, of which the leading ones are Presbyterian and Episcopalian. There are four banks, ten newspapers, and various societies, insurance offices, &c., &c. There is also a flourishing Medical College.

The HARBOR of Cleveland is one of the best on Lake Erie. It is formed by the mouth of Cuyahoga river, extended between two piers of stone masonry, 1300 feet in length, and 200 feet apart.

The RAILROAD STATION Houses are down near the Pier, on the shore. The Cincinnati Railroad extends, gradually, from the central plain of the State, through the valley of a little creek, till it reaches the Cuyahoga, and passes through the harbor part of the town.

The Station Houses of all the Railroads are at the same place—the Cincinnati, the Pittsburgh, the Wellsville, and the Lake Shore; by one or other of which lines, the traveller may take his departure for any place in the United States.

LAKE ERIE.—Before we begin a new departure, let us take a calm view of the beautiful Lake; for, beautiful it is, unless, indeed, irritated by a storm, when dark and lowering it casts an angry look upon all beholders. But if you leave Cleveland in a steamer, upon a moonlight evening, and wake to a sunlight morning, there is exceeding beauty upon the bosom of the Lake. We have looked out at evening, when dark clouds were gathered in the west, and here and there the lurid lightning played upon the scowling waters, and we thought, perhaps, the spirit of the Tempest was preparing for us all his wrath, and unloosing the winds upon the face of the Deep. Then we have waked, at daylight, and every element was hushed to sleep, and motion itself had almost ceased; calm was the silent waters, and placid as if never stirred, and the heavens were reflected, and the bright sunbeams glanced from their face. Far ahead a column of smoke revealed a steamer, wending her rapid way; far to the north, loomed up from the water the white sails of a schooner; and on our right was the sandy beach, and beyond, the green woods of Ashtabula. Such a scene is worth going far to see, and when you have sat and watched the eternal flow of Niagara, and gazed upon the rocky pass of the Highlands, you will, perhaps, think think that, however grand they may be, few things can so image forth the spirits of Peace and Beauty, as a sunrise on Lake Erie.

Roll on, thou deep and dark blue Erie—roll!

LITTLE MIAMI RAIL ROAD,

FROM CINCINNATI TO CLEVELAND.

	Distance from Cincinnati.	Intermediate Distance.	Distance from Cleveland.
Cincinnati			255
Cincinnati Engine House	3	3	252
Plainville	9½	6½	245½
Milford	14	4½	241
Loveland's	23	9	232
Foster's	27¼	4¼	227¾
Deerfield	32¼	5	222¾
Morrow	36½	4¼	218½
Fort Ancient	41½	5	213½
Freeport	45	3½	210
Corwin	50¾	5¾	204¼
Spring Valley	58	7¼	197
Xenia	65	7	190
Cedarville	73	8	182
Selma	79	6	176
South Charleston	84	5	171
London	95	11	160
West Jefferson	105½	10½	149½
Rome	112	6½	143
Columbus	120	8	135
Worthington	129	9	126
Orange	136	7	119
Berlin	140	4	115
Delaware	143	3	112
Eden	147	4	108
Ashley	151	4	104
Cardington	158	7	97
Gilead	163	5	92
Iberia	170	7	85
Galion	176	6	79
Vernon	180	4	75
Shelby	188	8	67
Salem	195	7	60
Greenwich	201	6	54
New London	208	7	47
Rochester	214	6	41
Wellington	219	5	36
La Grange	226	7	29
Grafton	230	4	25
Eaton	232½	2½	22½
Columbia	236½	4	18½
Olmsted	240	3½	15
Perea	242½	2½	12½
Rockport	248	5½	7
Cleveland	255	7	

CINCINNATI AND HILLSBOROUGH RAILROAD,
COMMENCING AT LOVELAND, ON THE LITTLE MIAMI RAILROAD.

	Distance from Loveland's	Intermediate Distance.	Distance from Hillsbro'
Loveland's			38½
Spence's Station	6½	6½	33
Goshen & Wilmington Turnpike.	10	3½	26½
Blanchester	16	6	20
Westboro'	20	4	16
Lynchburgh	26½	6½	10
Hoagland's	33	6½	6½
Hillsboro'.	38½	5½	

SANDUSKY, MANSFIELD AND NEWARK RAILROAD.

	To Newark.	Intermediate Distance.	From Newark.
Sandusky	0		116
Monroeville	16	16	100
Pontiac	20	4	96
Havana	24	4	92
Centreville	28	4	88
Plymouth	36	8	80
Shelby, [Junction]	45	9	71
Mansfield	56	11	60
Lexington	65	9	51
Belville	70	5	46
Independence	75	5	41
Frederick	86	11	30
Mt. Vernon	92	6	24
Utica	104	12	12
Nəwark	116	12	

NEW YORK AND ERIE RAIL ROAD.

LENGTH, from Pierpont to Dunkirk, 445 miles. ROUTE, from New York to Dunkirk, via Patterson, 460 miles.
USUAL TIME, from New York to Dunkirk, 20 hours.

Principal Stations.	Miles from N.York.	Fare.	Principal Stations.	Miles from Dunkirk	Fare.
NEW YORK,	0	$ cts.	DUNKIRK.	0	$ cts.
Piermont,	25	25	Dayton,	22	50
Suffern,*	32	60	Cattaraugus,	31	55
Turner's,	47	95	Little Valley,	38	75
Chester,†	55	1 00	Great Valley,	48	1 00
Goshen,	60	1 10	Allegany,	61	1 25
Middletown,	67	1 25	Olean,	65	1 30
Otisville,	75	1 50	Cuba,	79	1 55
Delaware,	88	1 75	Friendship,	86	1 75
Lackawaxen,	111	2 25	Hornellsville	127	2 50
Narrowsburgh,	122	2 40	Addison,	157	3 10
Hancock,	164	3 25	Painted Post,	167	3 30
Deposit,	177	3 50	CORNING,	168	3 35
Susquehannah,	192	3 85	ELMIRA,	187	3 75
Great Bend,‡	200	4 00	Waverley,	204	4 15
BINGHAMTON,	215	4 25	OWEGO,	223	4 50
Union,	223	4 45	Union,	237	4 80
OWEGO,§	237	4 75	BINGHAMTON,	245	5 00
Waverley,	256	5 15	Great Bend,	260	5 25
ELMIRA,‖	273	5 50	Susquehannah,	268	5 40
CORNING,¶	292	5 80	Deposit,	283	5 75
Painted Post,	293	5 85	Hancock,	296	
Addison,	303	6 00	Narrowsburgh,	338	6 75
Hornellsville,	333	6 60	Lackawaxen,	349	6 85
Friendship,	374	7 50	Delaware,	372	7 20
Cuba,	381	7 70	Otisville,	385	
Olean,	395	7 95	Middletown,	393	7 75
Allegany,	399	8 00	Goshen,	400	7 85
Great Valley,	412	8 00	Chester,	405	7 90
Little Valley,	422	8 00	Turner's,	413	8 00
Cattaraugus,	429	8 00	Suffern,	428	8 00
Dayton,	438	8 00	Piermont,	444	8 00
DUNKIRK.	4 60	8 00	NEW YORK.	460	8 00

* The Ramapo and Patterson, and Hudson River Railroad runs from this station to Jersey City, 32 miles,

† The Newburgh Branch Railroad runs from this station to Newburgh, 19½ miles.

‡ Lackawanna Railroad runs from this station to Scranton, Pa. 50 miles.

§ The Cayuga and Susquehanna Railroad runs from this station to Ithaca, 33 miles, connecting with steamers running on Cayuga Lake.

‖ The Chemung Railroad runs from Elmira to Jefferson, 21 miles, connecting with Steamers and Railroad, to Canandaigua, &c.

¶ The Corning and Blosburg Railroad runs from this station to Blosburg, Pa. 40 miles.

THE CINCINNATI GAZETTE,

Daily, $8.00, Tri-Weekly, $5.00, Weekly, $2 per annum.

THE HISTORY OF THE GAZETTE, AND THE CHANGES IN THE PAPER, THE PLACE, AND PEOPLE.

On the 25th of June, 1825, was commenced a new volume of the DAILY GAZETTE and of the LIBERTY HALL AND CINCINNATI WEEKLY GAZETTE. We deem it a fitting time to make some remarks as to the history of the paper, and the history of the North-West Territory, which has passed from a wilderness to a country of *States*, teeming with millions of population, and evidencing a prosperous and enlightened community.

On the 9th of November, 1793, the first newspaper was established in the North-West Territory, by Wm. Maxwell, and called the *Centinel of the North West Territory*, as it was indeed a wilderness, without the range of civilization, and within the land of savages. At the time of the establishment of this paper, Cincinnati was in the range of the Indians, and some are yet amongst us who, when their huts were building, watched the woods, rifle in hand, to keep the workmen from being scalped. Mr. Ferguson informs us, that whilst the choppers were cutting down the trees in the North-East part of the city to build his cabin, corner of Third and Main, he stood as sentinel, or ranged the forest rifle in hand. One of the Indians informed a citizen in after days, that he used to watch the movements of the early settlers from the limbs of the trees on Mount Adams.

The Cincinnati Gazette is a regular descendant by transfer of subscription list from this first paper, although the name and immediate papers are of subsequent date; the Gazette derives its name by original date to this day. In 1796, the original paper changed its name to Freeman's Journal, in consequence of the sale to E. Freeman. On the 28th May, 1799, the Western Spy and Hamilton Gazette was established, and on the 9th December, 1804, the publication of the Liberty Hall was commenced, a title still retained in our Weekly, and by which it is yet only known to many of our country readers. On the 15th July, 1815, T. Palmer commenced publishing the Gazette; but on the 11th December, 1815, he sold out and united with the Liberty Hall, and thereafter the paper was known as the Liberty Hall and Cincinnati Gazette. On the 25th June, 1827, this city, as yet had no Daily, though claiming a population of 19,000 people. It was suggested to the proprietors that a daily should be issued, and Messrs. E. Morgan and his co-partner canvassed the city to ascertain whether they could get patrons enough to sustain the enterprise, and having obtained in this population of 19,000 the number of 164 subscribers to a daily. they commenced publishing a Daily, under the abreviation of Daily Cincinnati Gazette, and it has continued till this day.

The Gazette has now subscribers who have been regular readers since the beginning. The changes which have been wrought in the country have been beyond those often witnessed by living men—the changes which have been wrought in the Gazette, its appearance, its news, its expenses, and its business, have been equally great. In the files of the Gazette will be found a history of the wilderness—the incoming of millions of people, and the most important events in our local history. Amongst the events, the beginning of which are noted, we may briefly state

The first paper issued.
First book published.
July 5, 1814, first Steamboat arrival announced,
March 3, 1816, first laying out of Covington.
1815, first steamboat built at Cincinnati launched.
Feb. 1, 1816, first Iron Foundery.
Aug. 1, 1816, first agitation of Gas works, by Wm. Greene.
Oct., 1818, first Circulating Library,
1819, first passenger steamer, Gen. Pike, built—100 feet keel, 14 state rooms, and provision for eighty-six passengers.
1839, first Free Soil paper issued.

The changes in proprietors and leading editors of the Gazette, considering the length of time it has been published, have been comparatively few. Prior to 1822, and for some years, Isaac G. Burnet, Esq. was editor, when he gave way to B. F. Powers, (brother of the sculptor,) who continued until 1825, when he was succeeded by Charles Hammond, who occupied the place, being almost sole editor, till his death, April 3, 1840, he was succeeded, at his request, made known before his death, by John C. Wright, the present senior editor.

With the change of times has come a change in the publisher's business, equally material—a change in the mode of getting news, a change in the amount of reading to satisfy an enlightened and commercial community, and a change in expense. Changes generally against the publisher, as the cost of a weekly paper, the cost of a daily paper, and the cost of an advertisement have continued the same; although many hundred per cent. of expense has been added. The original subscribers have always paid us their $2 for the Weekly, or their $8 for the Daily. Some of these changes it may be interesting to note.

We cannot go back into description further than 1804, when we find the *Liberty Hall*, issued from the cock-loft of a log-cabin, situated on the slope of the hill, about twenty feet above the present grade of the street, on the south-east corner of Sycamore and Third streets. The paper was royal size, and the entire work—editing, composition, press-work, distributing, mailing, and collecting, was chiefly done by Rev. Mr. Browne, the proprietor, with time to preach and do other jobs. The price of the paper was $2, the entire expense about $15. At this time, we find the latest news received, was from London, in three months, and from New York in one month. The favorite route East to the "Old Settlements," as the Atlantic was called by Mr. Ferguson, (still living,) was on horse-back, via Cumberland Gap and the Virginia Valley. The changes in style and expense have been continuous and constant.

On the 25th June, 1827, when the first Daily was begun, the facilities for news were not very great—New York was a great way off, and mails the only resource—slow and uncertain. The expenses of publication about $40 per week, and the size superroyal. In 1835, in order to show the change wrought, an entire paper of January 11, 1794, was transferred into the Gazette, and made then but four and one-fourth columns, or one-seventh of the then Daily. If a transfer were now made, the first Daily would not make much, if any, over one-seventh of the present Daily.

The change in the labor of getting up a paper has been equally great. At first, and even till about 1840, but one editor was necessary, and but few compositors. A job-office, necessary to keep, to attend to customers, as a distinct office would not pay for itself. The Gazette, not content with mails, was the first, as a regular part of their business—to run an express to obtain early news. It was continued till the telegraph annulled all such enterprises. The city changed so rapidly from a village to a great commercial mart, as to require a special City or Local Editor, and in 1842, John B. Russell was first detailed on this duty. Since then we have had to have a Commercial Editor, and this branch of expense embraces about one-fifth of all. We have now about 200 exchange papers, and require four Editors for foreign news and two City Editors.

For near one-fourth of a century a single hand press and a single pressman were all that were needed. In 1834, the first power press ever brought west of the mountains, we believe, was brought out by the Gazette, and in 1843 the first Hoe Cylinder Press for a daily paper. In early times the Gazette forms were locked and the paper off the press by early bed time—now there is no hour of the day or night that persons are not at work getting out the paper. At one o'clock, A. M., seven hands find employment at the *presses* whilst *one* used to answer.

Instead of using the cock-loft of a log cabin, with hand press and case to do the editing, composing, press work and distributing, we now have a six story building fully occupied—seven power presses at work—printing, press work, binding, engraving, &c., &c. done, 100 persons employed, and our expenses increased from $30 a week to over $150 per day.

Such are the changes in this feature of the business, and we may say to the patrons of the Gazette, that the quantity of matter for the same price has duplicated, and the ems of composition, the only test of the amount of reading—has changed since 1849 from 24,000 to 95,000. The Gazette furnishes materially more than any other of its cotemporaries. We find on examination that the city daily papers measure as follows:

Sun contains	85,000 ems.
Atlas	161,000 "
Nonpareil	187,000 "
Commercial	199,000 "
Times	220,000 "
Enquirer	224,000 "
Gazette	382,000 "

We are gratified to state that our business, our circulation and advertisements have never been greater or better than now. We have patrons who have stood by the office unwaveringly for half a century, and we may say, generally, that we rarely lose a subscriber, and that counting from months to months, as far back as our books are at hand to examine, we find we always have enlarged our list of subscribers, and our circle of advertisers; and the gain in our subscription list daily and weekly, and of advertisers, has been greater the past six months than ever before.

For the success which has attended our efforts—for the confidence and patronage of our friends, we are thankful. To those who are interested in the progress of this Establishment—to the fast friends, new and old, who feel an interest in us, we have believed that this statement was due, and that it might be interesting to others. We shall continue to move onward—always improving; always meeting the wishes in view of an enlightened community as far as possible; always advocating sound principles, and the interest of the city and the West; always promoting the Whig cause, as the cause of the country; but not as the follower of any man or men—not influenced by temporary excitements—not changing for local influences. We shall endeavor, as always, to pay respect to the opinions of others, and differing, to do so as may be due from gentlemen to gentlemen. Courteous to all—following the behests and dictations of none.

CINCINNATI, July 22, 1852.

NOTE.—This is one of the sections of the several Railroads of Ohio, which will be embraced in the Guide Book. It is purposed, as fast as the work can be got through the press, to embrace all the Railroads of the State of Ohio. The sketches of the greater number of the Roads are complete, and the others are progressing as fast as possible. The engraving and stereotyping consume much more time than was anticipated.

Should this book fall into the hands of any, who see errors in the facts stated, we shall be obliged for any correction. We shall, also, be grateful for any local incidents in the history of the country along the line of any of the Railroads in Ohio and Indiana, built or building.

www.ingramcontent.com/pod-product-compliance
Lightning Source LLC
LaVergne TN
LVHW050529100826
845148LV00002B/490